An Affair with My Mother

A story of adoption, secrecy and love

CAITRÍONA PALMER

PENGUIN
IRELAND

PENGUIN IRELAND

UK | USA | Canada | Ireland | Australia
India | New Zealand | South Africa

Penguin Ireland is part of the Penguin Random House group of companies
whose addresses can be found at global.penguinrandomhouse.com.

First published 2016

001

Typeset by Palimpsest Book Production Ltd, Falkirk, Stirlingshire
Printed in Great Britain by Clays Ltd, St Ives plc

A CIP catalogue record for this book is available from the British Library

ISBN : 978–1–844–88357–8

www.greenpenguin.co.uk

MIX
Paper from
responsible sources
FSC® C018179

Penguin Random House is committed to a
sustainable future for our business, our readers
and our planet. This book is made from Forest
Stewardship Council® certified paper.

For my parents, Liam and Mary, with undying
love and gratitude.

For Sarah – and every birth mother burdened by secrecy
– that love and compassion may set you free.

And for Dan, who has given me the greatest gift of all.

Author's Note

By agreeing to share her story with me for this book, my birth mother took a tremendous leap of faith and courage. As she wishes to remain anonymous, I have changed her name and changed or suppressed certain potentially identifying details – and those of some others, including my biological father.

Prologue

It's hard to know what to wear when you're meeting your mother for the first time.

After some deliberation I chose dark denim trousers, a fitted black jacket and low black heels, with minimal make-up and simple jewellery. Reviewing myself in the mirror that Saturday morning, I felt satisfied. Ready for business, my reflection said. Ready for anything.

My adoptive father – the man I've always known simply as Dad – offered to drive me into town. I wanted time alone on the train to listen to my Walkman and prepare, but a heavy rain started to fall and so I relented. By the time we pulled up outside Number 82, Haddington Road, a Georgian house near the Grand Canal, I was sweating and felt nauseous.

Dad, never big on displays of emotion, patted me gently on the hand.

'I can wait here if you'd like,' he said softly. 'No problem at all.'

'You're fine, Dad,' I said, reaching over to kiss him gently on the cheek, 'you head off. I'll be OK.'

Dad waited, his yellow hazard lights flashing, as I climbed the granite steps towards the door. As the door opened, I turned and bent down to see his face as he drove off. Our eyes met and he waved. I had never loved him more than I did in that moment. At the same time, I felt like a traitor. The worst daughter in the world.

Catherine, the social worker assigned to my case, welcomed me and led me to her office upstairs. It appeared that

I was the first to arrive. We sat and made small talk over steaming mugs of milky tea. A plate of plain biscuits lay on the table in front of me, but one glance in their direction made my stomach lurch. I tried to focus on what Catherine was saying while suppressing the urge to vomit and looking around the room for the nearest wastebasket.

Outside I heard the slam of a car door, then footsteps. The doorbell rang. Snatches of hushed conversation drifted upwards from the hallway. Catherine smiled kindly, patted me on the arm and left the room. *Showtime*, I thought to myself. I sat alone, staring at the crucifix hanging on the opposite wall and wondering if I could still make it to the bathroom.

I wanted my mother – and not the one that I was about to meet. I had left Mam an hour earlier, enveloped in the warmth of her kitchen in north Dublin, standing over the electric cooker immersed in her Saturday ritual of making vegetable soup and soda bread. I wanted to tell her that I was sorry, that this was all a big mistake, a foolish fumble at finding my identity that had got out of control. I wanted things to be normal again.

But an echo of footsteps in the corridor told me it was too late. I looked down at my feet and forced a smile. Catherine stepped in, followed by a woman wearing an oversized fake-fur coat. Seeing me, the woman put her hands to her face and gasped. She rushed towards me, the metallic bangles she was wearing on her long arms clashing and clanging as she reached out. She smelt of cheap perfume and wore too much blush. She grabbed me, pulling me to her, sobbing. I hugged her, patting her on the back, wishing she would let me go.

'Caitríona, Caitríona, Caitríona,' she said, repeating my name over and over, sobbing.

I said nothing. I felt nothing.

'I'll leave you both to it then,' I heard Catherine say.

'Don't go,' I wanted to scream at her. 'Please don't go. Stay. Stay here with me, please. Don't leave me alone with this woman.'

I

The painting called to me in the darkness.

I had begun to anticipate it every night when, racked with insomnia, I would slip quietly out of the bed that I shared with my boyfriend to pad across the black and white tiles of our kitchen to the back window of our apartment, which overlooked the bulky silhouette of Boston Medical Center. There, I would lean my cheek against the cool of the wall and stare out across the rooftops. In a four-storey brownstone house directly behind ours, beyond the black outline of a fire escape, the same third-floor light was always on. It illuminated, on the wall of what appeared to be a living room, a gold-framed portrait of a woman. Her skin was luminous, pearled against the darkness. The dim light made the room look intimate, inviting, secure. I'd got in the habit of looking into that room on my nocturnal wanderings, imagining who lived in the house, wishing somehow that it was me. For twenty minutes or so I would stand at the window until a chill took over, returning then to bed, feeling empty and unnerved, frustrated by an emotional itch that I could neither locate nor explain.

It was the autumn of 1998 and I was twenty-six years old. For months I had been assailed by anxiety and foreboding, a feeling that I was somehow incomplete. The source of this feeling was a mystery to me. I was living the life that I had always dreamt of. I had recently secured a position with an organization called Physicians for Human Rights (PHR), working with forensic scientists, doctors, lawyers and former aid workers, and I loved it. My British boyfriend and I had, over the course of a year and a half, cobbled together a happy existence in our newspaper-strewn South End apartment. I loved Chris's brilliant mind and the nimble way he had of making me laugh. I had never been happier in a relationship and was very much in love.

That September, I tried to explain away my nocturnal anxieties as a symptom of another, more concrete problem: with my student visa about to expire, I had been given a month by the immigration authorities to leave the United States. Hoping to stop the wheels of deportation, I conducted a frenzied charm offensive, getting politicians in the US and Ireland to write to the immigration authorities asking them to extend my visa. But the INS wasn't budging. The scholarship that had brought me to America had a rule stipulating that I leave after two years, no matter what. It didn't matter that I was in love or had a job. I had to go. The only question was where.

The answer turned out to be Bosnia – and that was not as unlikely as it might sound. After completing my studies at Boston College in the summer of 1997, I'd taken a short-term job in Sarajevo, working in the headquarters of a European organization tasked with monitoring the tenuous peace that had followed the savage civil war. I had told Chris – ever patient – that I would be back in three months. In the end I stayed away for six. During those months living in Sarajevo, I felt more alive than I had in years. I wore a white military uniform, took orders from a Dutch general and drank way too much in the local Irish pub perched on a hill overlooking the city. My friends were diplomats, peacekeepers and young Bosnian artists who mesmerized me with their stories of survival during the siege. It felt to me that I was at the centre of the world.

Knowing of my Sarajevo sojourn, PHR's director responded to the news of my impending deportation by suggesting that I relocate to their office in Bosnia. There, a small team of forensic scientists was overseeing the exhumation of hundreds of mass graves left after the war and attempting to determine the fate of over 7,500 missing men and boys from the UN safe haven of Srebrenica, which had been overrun by Serb forces four years earlier. It wasn't clear what role I would play, but my work for PHR consisted largely of writing press releases and reports, and there was a view that the Bosnia office – struggling to keep up with the influx of media enquiries that came with the discovery of each new grave – needed help on the communications front.

Chris and I discussed the offer and agreed that moving to Bosnia with PHR was my best hope of getting back into America on a work visa in two years' time. Marriage was the other, more obvious, possibility, but that option hung in the air untouched.

I left Boston in October 1998. As I stepped off the Swissair plane and on to the tarmac, Sarajevo seemed less alluring than the place I remembered from the year before. The steep hills of the city's piney valley were shrouded in a soupy fog and a layer of grime coated the bullet-scarred apartment blocks of the New Town. Flashing my passport at a bored policeman at passport control, I collected my bag from the floor of the arrivals hall and went out to wait for the PHR staff member sent to fetch me. Moments later, my suitcase having been thrown into the back of a white pickup truck normally used to ferry corpses from the mass graves to the morgue, we set off down Sniper Alley. I was told that I would have to report to the PHR office in Tuzla, in eastern Bosnia, in two days.

I look back on that scene now – sitting high in the cab of

a pickup truck, trying desperately to make a good impression on a new colleague – and feel almost sorry for myself. I was so naive in that moment, so full of trust and confidence. I had no idea what was waiting for me in the weeks and months ahead.

Shortly before I arrived, PHR colleagues in Tuzla had helped in the discovery and exhumation of a mass grave in Glumina, a town near the Serbian border in eastern Bosnia.

The grave at Glumina was fifty-one metres long and nine metres wide. Two hundred and seventy-four victims, Bosnian Muslims ranging in age from 14 to 80, all but two of them male and all dressed in civilian clothing, were arranged in two parallel rows, their heads pointing south. Most had been shot in the head, a dozen or so bludgeoned to death. Three had suffered broken necks, possibly the result of strangulation.

The pit at Glumina was the largest mass grave discovered up to that point in Bosnia, and it was big news. I had spent my last days in the Boston office fielding calls about it from Reuters, the *New York Times* and the *Boston Globe*. On the phone with PHR's forensic scientists in the field in Bosnia, I'd learned new words like 'saponified' – used to describe a corpse that has become waxy. I remember cheerfully telling the journalists that if they called me in a few days' time I'd be able to give them a first-hand account of the Glumina grave.

Driving towards the morgue in Tuzla on my first morning on the job, the prospect didn't seem so cheerful. My communications director in Boston urged me to go down to the morgue, get some quotes from family members and local officials and write up a press release on PHR's efforts to identify the dead. Up till then, my interactions with the remains had taken place within the softly lit confines of

Dublin funeral homes, standing over the embalmed remains of elderly relatives and neighbours who had slipped off peacefully in their sleep, or at the end of a long illness, their bodies wrapped in silky shrouds, their hands clutching rosary beads. Now the term 'mass grave', which I had bandied about so liberally in the weeks before my departure for Tuzla, didn't seem so abstract. Nothing prepared me for the stench and sight of nearly three hundred rotting corpses laid out in the car park of the local morgue, their mouths agape, their skin peat-brown and leathery. Circling the lines of corpses underneath a persistent drizzle were dozens of weary-looking family members who had been bused in from all parts of Bosnia to participate in this grotesque identity parade. I watched in fascination as a female forensic anthropologist wearing white latex gloves reached into the mouth of a male corpse and gently pulled back his upper lip to reveal two broken teeth. A young woman searching for her husband collapsed in recognition.

Back at the office later that day, I couldn't shake off the image of that crumpled young widow. Nor could I rid my clothes and hair of the stench of decomposing flesh. The smell – nauseatingly sweet, like the blast from a New York dumpster brimming with rotten meat on a steaming summer's day – seemed permanently stuck to my body. It followed me everywhere. Each time I swallowed, I tasted decaying human flesh. That afternoon, I had to leave the kitchen to quietly retch in a nearby bathroom when a male colleague, just in the door from the Glumina identifications, sat in front of me and munched noisily on a salami and mayonnaise sandwich.

March 1999. It is just before dawn when I wake, and still dark outside. I lie in bed for a few moments, letting my eyes adjust to the shapes and contours of the room.

The vague but persistent hum of anxiety that I felt in Boston has followed me to Bosnia and, over the course of six months, intensified. This creeping, nameless preoccupation has taken the form of an uneasy energy, an unfathomable urge to run.

I am not a runner. If anything, I am the quintessential anti-runner, the disdainful sloth who just doesn't *get* the whole jogging thing – the rising early on weekday mornings to squeeze in a run before work, the pursuit of the endorphin rush. My grandfather, a stoic veteran of the First World War, always maintained that human beings were designed to walk, not run, a philosophy I adopted as my own.

But here I am, in the murky darkness of a frigid Balkan morning, pulling on an old tracksuit and lacing up my trainers. I slip out of my room, taking care not to tread on the squeaky bottom step of the rickety staircase that might disturb my sleeping housemate. I unlock the front door and step out on to the narrow pavement that snakes around the back of my landlord's house to the muddy street out front.

The street where I live and work remains unpaved. It is pockmarked with giant holes, many of which are filled with icy brown water from recent snowfalls. I jump over those that I know and curse when my foot lands in others I've forgotten.

My route takes me past the kiosk at the end of the street, the source of the delicious salty bread rolls that I buy every day for lunch and the backdrop to impromptu early-evening soccer games when my colleagues and I kick a ball around with the local kids. It snakes downhill to the left, past some open dumpsters, out on to a wide highway that circles the city limits. This street is now completely empty, illuminated here and there by giant steel street lamps that cast a sickly yellow light through the gloomy morning fog.

The main PHR office in Tuzla is located in a large house on Pere Ćuskića, a tiny residential road that divides the city from the lush hills of eastern Bosnia. My boss and other foreign staff live on the uppermost floors, surrounded by depressingly dark baroque furniture and tacky furnishings. Downstairs, in the basement, sits the nerve centre of the PHR operation – a busy office staffed with over a dozen employees.

Next door to the main office is a neat little house owned by a softly spoken widow whose son and daughter are employed by PHR. The top floor of this little house is occupied by PHR's Identification Project, where post-mortem information from the mass graves of eastern Bosnia is picked over and analysed in the hope of finding a positive match for a desperate family. Despite its depressing workload, the office is a cheerful place, staffed by a team of dedicated experts who share a taste for the macabre and a love of Turkish coffee and pungent local cigarettes.

I live in a large house next door. On the top floor of this building live several of PHR's forensic scientists, an eccentric bunch of anthropologists and pathologists. On winter evenings I am careful to avoid their work boots, scattered haphazardly in a large pile on the mat in the main entrance to the hallway, still slick with mud and the sickly-sweet scent of decomposing flesh.

Sarajevo, my first Bosnian home, is an elegant city nestled within a dramatic valley. Tuzla, by contrast, is a dump. For starters, the place literally stinks. Enormous squat smoke-stacks dominate the skyline, belching massive clouds of grey coal smoke that hang low over the red-tiled roofs. The smog fills my nostrils and causes my throat to ache. Even the ground under our feet is untrustworthy: the city sits atop massive salt deposits, and the extraction of these deposits over the years has caused some streets to buckle and warp above the shifting ground. The undulating roads and giant potholes elicit long and inventive curses from my Bosnian colleagues on our daily trips to the local morgue.

I jog past the Tuzla Commemorative Centre, the depository for the city's dead and the hub of PHR's missing-persons operations. It is a nondescript place, a rundown collection of single-storey buildings that sit behind a rusting white iron fence. In the car park, weeds grow tall between the cracks where PHR's white pickup trucks sit next to boxy old Mercedes hearses, the vehicles of choice for ferrying Tuzla's dead to the cemeteries on the outskirts of the city. At the rear of the property, set into the side of a grassy hill, sit two disused salt-mining tunnels, approximately fifteen feet wide and two hundred feet long. Accessed through heavy padlocked gates, their musty interiors are lit by long fluorescent tubes. Inside, the entire length of each tunnel is lined with four-tiered wooden shelves. On every available space, in filthy white plastic body bags, lie hundreds and hundreds of exhumed corpses.

After six months on the job I feel as though I have come a long way. Although my heart still races every time I approach an open body bag, I no longer gag when viewing its contents. As the person responsible for drawing the world's attention to PHR's exhumation and identification projects, I have become adept at whisking visiting journalists and dignitaries through the macabre tour of the various projects – the morgue, the tunnels and the 'de-fleshing room', a tiled chamber in the morgue where men in rubber overalls extract bits of bodies from the body bags, place them in long wire-mesh trolleys and blast them with powerful water hoses in an attempt to clean the bones for easier identification and storage.

No, it's not the dead who are bothering me, I realize, but

those left behind – the families of the missing, racked with madness and grief, searching for their loved ones. These people intimidate and scare me. They gather in angry groups around Tuzla, haranguing local officials for more information about the exhumation process, pleading for access to the remains.

I have no right to compare myself to the grief-stricken families of Bosnia's missing, but there is something in their wild-eyed desire to fill in the missing pieces that feels oddly familiar. Now, as I jog across this grey city, I access some fresh awareness of the pain of not knowing; the pain of feeling, day in and day out, that someone is missing.

As the dawn light breaks through the Tuzla smog, my morning run is nearing its end. I make my way back up the main highway, past the glassy walled exterior of the Hotel Tuzla and up the hill to the bumpy potholed street where I live and work. For the first time in weeks the incessant chatter inside my brain has ceased and I realize that there is something I need to do. After a hot shower, and a quick breakfast of espresso and toast, I make my way to my office in the adjacent house and shut the door.

I turn on my desk light and open my work diary, turning to the back page, where, months ago, I jotted down a telephone number. A quick mental calculation tells me that it's too early to phone Dublin.

A couple of hours later I pick up the phone and dial.

2

The home in which I grew up was abundant with love and affection, a place of clean sheets, sparkling countertops and nutritious home-cooked meals. Walking in the front door of our house, one was usually met by the aroma of freshly baked brown bread or a sugared apple tart straight out of the oven. The kitchen, which looked out on to our tidy back garden, was brightly lit and cosy, and the kettle was always on. It was a happy home; but it was also an Irish home very much of its time, which is to say that it was not the scene of much genuine emotional intimacy. My parents were efficiently undemonstrative, leaving the tears, the hugging and the grand gestures to the characters that we watched every night in British soap operas. So it is apt that my mother chose a time when we were engrossed in a chore, with very little opportunity for eye contact, to tell me that I was not her biological child.

It was my sixth birthday, a Wednesday afternoon, and my mother and I were making my bed. I was standing on one side, next to the window, Mam on the far side in the narrow aisle that separated my bed from the one where my older sister, Thérèse, slept. Across the room, on a dresser covered with a delicate lace cloth, lay assorted treasures of our childhood: a china perfume dispenser with hand-painted flowers, a tiny replica of Michelangelo's Pietà and, in the middle, a glow-in-the-dark statue of the Virgin Mary, nearly a foot high, that my sister had picked up on a recent pilgrimage to Lourdes.

On Mam's count of three we lifted the sheets, as we had done countless times before, and watched as they billowed above our heads then floated down and settled back into place on the bed. The sun was streaming through the window, and I remember feeling incandescently happy. There was a birthday party at the weekend to look forward to, with games of pass-the-parcel and musical chairs, bottles of 7-Up and Fanta, and a sponge cake with freshly whipped cream, jam and pink icing. That night, my family would gather at the kitchen table to celebrate my birthday with my favourite meal, steak and onions baked in thick gravy with boiled potatoes and frozen peas. Soon Dad would be home, parking in our narrow concrete driveway, a Tea Time Express cake sitting in a box on the passenger seat beside him.

With my little hands I diligently smoothed the sheets and tucked them in neatly. My pillowcase depicted the orphaned Paddington Bear, his red duffel coat bearing a tag that read, 'Please look after this bear. Thank you.'

As Mam briskly smoothed out the bedspread, she began to talk.

'You know how it is your birthday today? Well, there is somebody very special that you need to say a prayer for.' I nodded obediently, not comprehending.

'You know how Mammy and Daddy have always told you how special you are? How we chose you especially to come and live with us? Well, before you were born, another mammy carried you in her tummy but was unable to keep you. She gave you to us and ever since on your birthday, and other special days, we have said a prayer for her. Now that you're a big girl I want you to remember her yourself and to pray for her, particularly on your birthday.'

The first pangs of an anxiety that would haunt me for the rest of my life began to spread across my gut. All of a sudden I felt unsure of my place in the world. I was not who I thought I was. There had been somebody else, another parent, a long time before, but she had given me away. Why would she do that? Was there something wrong with me? And if I had been given away once before then surely that could happen again? Fear began to creep into my mind.

I sat on the end of the bed as Mam held my hand. I remember looking out of the window at the canopy of the ash tree on the street below, trying to understand. I wanted to cry but worried that Mam would take my tears the wrong way; that she would think I was sad that I was not with the other woman – whoever she was. I had a million questions but was too shy to ask.

My mother's birthday revelation was a shock to the system, and yet it was not a complete surprise. Mam had told me many times before, albeit cryptically, that I was 'special'. During get-togethers with extended family I had seen furtive glances and heard the words 'adoption' and 'the natural mother'. But this, now, was something more concrete and dramatic: my mother telling me that I was not, in fact, her flesh and blood; that there was another woman, a woman who had given me away. A mother – *my* mother – who for no apparent reason had handed me over to a pair of complete strangers. A ghost for whom, on special occasions, I was now being asked to pray.

That was the day when my identity fractured and a dull emptiness established itself in my gut. I was now two people: the people-pleasing adoptee, ever fearful of being sent back; and the melancholy inner child locked in a quest to locate that missing part of me. Who was I? Where had I come from? I was an imposter, expected to continue living happily with one family having just been told that I came from another.

My thoughts were quickly dominated by this mythical mother, the one who had given me away. The villain or the victim, depending on my mood. She loomed constantly in my mind, this airy creature – beautiful, self-assured and fabulously successful. She took me out for ice cream and Coca-Cola, allowed me to eat candyfloss and chewing gum – delicacies forever denied to me by Mam and Dad – and let me stay up late to watch TV. She bought me a pony and cheered as I won rosettes in show-jumping competitions across Ireland, beaming in the stands as I beat kids from the posher parts of Dublin. She was glamorous, sophisticated, outrageously funny. She was the perfect mother, the envy of the playground, my greatest advocate and my biggest fan. This person was real and alive and tangible in every sense except the most important: she didn't exist.

Adoption was far from the minds of Liam and Mary Palmer when they began their married life together in a hastily built housing estate in north Dublin in July 1961.

They had fallen in love not quite two years earlier, having been introduced by my mother's brother Bill Wyse, an avid swimmer who knew Liam Palmer as a familiar face at a gentlemen's swimming hole, the Forty Foot, on the south side of Dublin Bay. Most evenings after work, rain or shine, Liam would hop on a bus or train out of the city centre and make his way to this rocky promontory. In the concrete bathing shelter that looked out on to the Irish Sea, Liam would change into a pair of swimming shorts and plunge into the frigid waters.

It was a bank holiday Sunday in August 1959, after an early-afternoon swim, when Bill – who was soon to enter the priesthood – invited my father to the modest terraced house in Terenure where he lived with his family. At the dining-room table, piled high with ham sandwiches and hot scones, Liam sat opposite Bill's younger sister, Mary, the only girl in the Wyse family. He could not take his eyes off her. Towards the evening's end, Mary mentioned an upcoming dance, a fundraiser for a local hospice. Liam saw his chance. The dance, which took place a couple of weeks later, became the first of many dates.

The Ireland in which Liam and Mary conducted their romance was economically impoverished and socially conservative. Liam and Mary came from devout Catholic families and conducted their courtship accordingly, spending a lot of time in the chaperoned living rooms of their respective childhood homes. They went to Mass most mornings, performed the devotions on every First Friday and attended weekly Expositions of the Sacred Sacrament and confession. Well-thumbed copies of the *Messenger of the Sacred Heart* sat on their kitchen tables. On weekends and some evenings after work, Liam would call at Mary's house, a twenty-minute walk from his home in Crumlin, and escort his sweetheart by bus into the city centre. At the Savoy Theatre on O'Connell Street, for 2/6 apiece, Liam would buy tickets to see the latest films from America and the UK. Around payday, Liam might splurge and take Mary to see Gilbert and Sullivan musicals in the Gaiety Theatre, just off Grafton Street. On some weekends during football season, Mary would join Liam and his twin brother, James, in the terraced stadium at Milltown to cheer on Shamrock Rovers. Liam, though a poor dancer himself, indulged Mary's love of dancing, taking her to a ballroom where a live showband played quicksteps, tangos and old-time waltzes.

They became engaged on 11 February 1960, a mere six months after they had first met. On the day of the engagement there was a big celebration in the Wyse family home, a high tea presided over by my maternal grandparents at which the two families officially met for the first time. My grandmother, Elizabeth, served tea and sandwiches, and bottles of lemonade were opened to toast the happy couple. A large cake, prominent in the centre of the table, completed the spread.

The ring was bought a couple of weeks later in a small jewellery shop on South Anne Street. Liam had saved assiduously for the purchase, and it showed. The ring was a dazzler: three diamonds set in yellow gold, a lavish gift for his bride-to-be and a sure sign that the couple were on their way up in the world. Now, with a wedding to plan and a house to buy, the trips to the Gaiety began to dwindle. Liam, a clerk in the payroll office of a rail and shipping company, had a well-paid and pensionable job, but still had to scrimp and save hard for a deposit to buy a house. Mary also had a good job, as a clerical officer for Bord na Móna. But there was a catch: her employment was subject to the 'marriage ban', under which she would be required to relinquish her position upon getting married. The rationale for the ban was ostensibly economic – the premise being that there were not enough jobs to allow some households to have two breadwinners – but it is no coincidence that the ban chimed perfectly with the social mores of the time and even with the Irish constitution, which stated (and still states) that 'the State recognizes that by her life within the home, woman gives to the State a support without which the common good cannot be achieved'.

By the end of the year, Liam and Mary had saved enough money for a deposit on a house. Mary wanted to stay south of the River Liffey, where they had both been raised. Liam, more adventurous, was willing to go further afield. One weekend, they visited a work colleague of Liam's in his newly built home in the north-eastern suburb of Raheny. During their courtship my parents had sometimes ventured north, taking the train out to Howth, a little fishing village perched beneath a gorse-strewn hill. There Liam and Mary would walk hand in hand down the pier and eat ice creams on a wall overlooking the harbour. Despite the charms of Howth, a move to the north side seemed out of the question until that Sunday afternoon when the couple walked into the gleaming new home of Liam's friend. The house was a modern marvel: a two-storey, three-bedroomed semi-detached with an attached garage and small gardens front and back. It was a veritable palace, particularly to Liam, who had started his life sharing two rooms in a house in the inner city with his parents and four brothers. To Mary, the kitchen in the new house was like a bright, modern dream. Before long, she and Liam paid £2,000 for a house in the same estate, Number 49. The house had a pebble-dashed front and wrought-iron gates that led to a small concrete driveway for the car that the couple still yearned to buy.

Liam and Mary married on 26 July 1961 at the Church of the Holy Rosary in Harold's Cross. The day before, Mary's mother buried a faded statue of the Infant of Prague in her back garden; according to superstition, this guaranteed good weather on the day of a wedding. The following day was sunny, but windy: a photograph from that morning shows Mary standing outside the church door, clasping her left hand to her veil, whipped up in the air by a sudden gust. She is laughing, her long slender right arm clutching a bouquet of delicate white orchids. Liam, handsome in a rented dark morning suit, stands to her left, smiling shyly, his hand on the door of the black limousine that will take them to their wedding reception. They look elated, hopeful, a little scared.

In keeping with Irish tradition at that time, the wedding ceremony was held at 9 a.m., necessitating a pre-dawn preening session for the bride and her two attendants. The Mass, presided over by Father Colum O'Donnell, the priest rolled out for all the Wyse clan's religious occasions, was sung in Latin, the traditional liturgy that would be abandoned a few years later as part of the Vatican II reforms. The bride wore white, a sumptuous gown of heavy satin overlain with delicate Carrickmacross lace. The dress, made by a friend of Mary's, was a clever rip-off: a duplicate of an expensive gown that Mary had seen in an elegant Dublin department store but lacked the funds to buy. Mary's two bridesmaids – her best friend from work, Anne Hammil, and my father's sister Carmel – wore lemon taffeta gowns and carried bouquets of roses. The best man was Liam's brother James, a slender, tall man with a shock of wiry black hair who bore little physical resemblance to his shorter red-haired twin.

The couple, breaking from the tradition of holding a small reception in the home of the bride, chose the Salthill Hotel in Dún Laoghaire as the setting for their wedding 'breakfast' – a turkey and ham lunch in the hotel dining room for sixty or so guests, followed by an afternoon of music and dancing. Waiters in black bow ties served guests from stainless-steel platters. There was a three-tiered wedding fruit cake covered in layers of sweet marzipan and hard sugared icing, decorated with a silver-papered horseshoe for good luck. In the garden of the hotel, amid blooming rose bushes and hydrangeas, a local photographer corralled the happy wedding party into a huddle, the bride and groom in the middle, their parents on either side. Those photographs are the only pictures I have of my Wyse and Palmer grandparents together, awkward in their stiff woollen suits and smiling timidly at the camera.

The bride and groom, suited up in smart 'going away' clothes, left the party in a rush just after lunch, bound for

Amiens Street station and the three o'clock train to Belfast. From Belfast they caught a ferry to Heysham and then a train to the southern English port of Dover. (Dad cannot recollect why they took such a roundabout route.) They then sailed on to the French port of Calais and took a train to Paris, where they spent the first two proper nights of their marriage in a little hotel near the Champs-Élysées. From Paris they travelled to the pilgrimage town of Lourdes, in the Pyrenees, where the Virgin Mary is said to have appeared to a fourteen-year-old girl in 1858. They spent a week there, good pilgrims who happened to be on their honeymoon, before crossing the Spanish border to the town of San Sebastián. There, Liam picked up a horrendous case of food poisoning, cementing Mam's deep hostility towards non-Irish food, aka 'foreign muck'.

When the honeymooners returned to Dublin they moved straight into Number 49. The estate was still being built around them, the road unpaved and multiple houses along the street incomplete. But despite the noise of the cement mixers and the bags of gravel stacked outside their front gate, the couple were starry-eyed over their new home. The walls were papered, the doors, windows and trim freshly painted, the linoleum flooring in the kitchen and bathroom neatly laid. The new furniture, bought as wedding gifts by relatives and friends, was arranged carefully on the still-uncarpeted floors. Visiting relatives clucked and cooed over the wedding china in the cherry cabinets, the new sofa and chairs in the living room, the fancy electric stove in the kitchen. A blessing of their marriage from Pope John XXIII hung on the kitchen wall. Next to it was another wedding gift, a picture of Christ, his eyes downcast, his head pinched by a crown of thorns, his hand gesturing sadly towards a bleeding open heart. Underneath the picture was a small red lamp, a flickering flame that paid eternal homage to the

Sacred Heart. As a child, the glow of that red electric light both comforted and unnerved me – a welcoming sight on gloomy wintry mornings but also a constant reminder that Jesus was always watching.

In the months leading up to the wedding Liam was relocated from the company headquarters at Dublin port to a position at the flagship travel office in the city centre. The new job meant more pay, a happy coincidence for a young man burdened with a hefty new mortgage. For the next six years he worked out of this storefront office, booking passengers on the mail boat from Dublin to the Welsh port of Holyhead, making reservations for them on the connecting train to London. The vast majority of the passengers were the Irish unemployed – tens of thousands of young men and women desperate to find work in Britain. Taking their cash and stamping their tickets, my father felt complicit in this national mass exodus, playing a part in exporting fellow Irishmen and women less fortunate than he.

While Liam took the train or bus every morning into the office on Westmoreland Street, Mary stayed behind in Number 49, jobless for the first time since leaving school. While Liam was at work, Mary cleaned, shopped for groceries and hung the laundry out to dry on the nylon clothes line that ran through the middle of the narrow grassy back garden. She made friends with the neighbours (including other women consigned to their homes by the marriage ban), popping in and out of their homes to share a cup of tea and to catch up on the neighbourhood news. And she cooked dinner: roast meats, potatoes and boiled vegetables. On summer evenings she'd prepare a salad, arranging leaves of delicate butter lettuce next to tomatoes, pickled beetroot and thick slices of ham. On the table would be a springy loaf of white bread, cut in large slices and served with salty butter. On the way home from the bus stop, Liam would pause at the local shop and buy the evening newspaper. Then they'd sit together at the dinner table, washing the food down with strong tea, listening to the news on the radio and catching up on the day's events.

Mary became pregnant early in 1963, and in October gave birth to a girl, Thérèse. In May 1966, she bore a son, David. And five years later, during the summer of 1971, Mary became pregnant again. In the interim Liam had been promoted once more and was now working at the cargo terminal in Dublin port, a short drive along the coastal road from Number 49. Liam and Mary had made modest but discernible improvements to the house – there were new carpets on the floor, venetian blinds in the windows. The gardens out front and back boasted rose bushes and purple hydrangeas. A new car sat in the driveway. My parents were excited about this latest pregnancy, a summer surprise. Thérèse was particularly enthralled by the prospect of a new baby and hoped it was a girl.

After lunch on the afternoon of Sunday 26 September, while my father watched the All-Ireland football final on a new black-and-white television, my mother was struck with a sudden abdominal pain that worsened through the evening. By nightfall a doctor was called to the house. Seeing that my mother was gravely ill and suspecting a ruptured ectopic pregnancy, the doctor telephoned one of Dublin's main maternity hospitals to demand that she be admitted immediately. While the administrator on the other end of the phone dithered about available beds, the doctor lost his cool. 'I will hold you responsible for her life,' he yelled down the line as he gestured frantically to Liam to place Mary in his car.

That night at the hospital, the surgeons worked furiously

to stem the bleeding. The following morning my mother, weak from multiple blood transfusions, was told that the pregnancy was lost, the damage to her reproductive organs severe. There would be no more babies.

Stunned by this new reality, my mother and father sat in the hospital ward and discussed their next step. Even though she was too weak to sit up, and even though she had barely had time to absorb the loss of her pregnancy, Mary floated the idea of adopting. That afternoon, Thérèse and David were brought into the hospital. Thérèse, eight years old and confused by the course of events, asked to see the new baby. Mary, grief-stricken but encouraged by the conversation that she had just had with Liam, knew exactly what to say.

'We have no baby right now,' she gently told my sister, 'but we will have one very soon. I can promise you that.'

When I made the phone call to St Patrick's Guild, the Catholic agency in Dublin that had brokered my adoption twenty-seven years before, I did so from my little office on the second floor of PHR's identification house. The room was tiny, perhaps eight feet by ten, but I loved its cosy confines. The floor was covered with a bright patchwork rug that I had bought at a local craft shop. On the wall, next to a bookcase stacked with PHR reports and the volumes of poetry I'd brought with me from Boston, hung a bright red and purple tapestry. On the desk, beneath the soft glow of a lamp that I had picked up for next to nothing at a local flea market, sat framed pictures of Chris and my family. The small window to the right of my desk overlooked another house and the office where my boss, Laurie, sat. Often, during the workday, we would wave to each other. Sometimes, if I craned my neck hard enough, I could catch a glimpse of the garden in front of the house, dotted with plum trees that yielded fat purple fruit in the summer. I loved walking into this office, turning on the lamp and quietly settling down to work. It was an escape from the filth and stench of the morgue and I felt quietly productive there, sending dispatches back to Boston and the world beyond about the depressing and mounting tally of the Srebrenica dead.

It was also from this office that I called my parents in April 1999 to tell them that I had decided to search for my birth mother. Having made contact with the adoption agency weeks before, I delayed the call to Liam and Mary, dreading the moment when I would have to share the news. I was most apprehensive about telling Mam, fearful that she would see my search as a rejection of her, as a deliberate quest to replace my mother. But there was no other option: long ago I had decided that skulking behind my parents' backs would not do. Weeks before, I had called Thérèse and David to sound them out. 'Can't you just do it quietly without them knowing?' my brother had asked.

'There's no way,' I had told him. 'It would be far, far worse when they did find out.'

The delay in phoning home was not entirely of my own making. That month my workload at PHR had surged dramatically, the result of a new war that was brewing 400 kilometres away in Kosovo. Our forensic scientists were still literally knee-deep in the mass graves of Bosnia, and now we were hearing of fresh atrocities – killings, beatings, torture and sexual assault. During the same week in March that I called St Patrick's Guild, Serb troops had begun massing on the border of Kosovo in a new campaign to cleanse the ethnic Albanian population. By late March a NATO-led air war had begun. Sitting at my desk in Tuzla I heard the roar of jets overhead as they made their way across the border to bomb targets in Kosovo and Serbia. The mood in the office was tense and desolate. 'I can't believe this is happening again,' was the phrase I heard most often amongst my Bosnian colleagues that month.

When I did finally make the call, I was relieved to hear my father pick up the phone. As a child, I had always come to Dad first with bad news. During my schooldays, afflicted with a profound inability to understand maths, I would wait to seek him out in the quiet of the evening so that I could slip him yet another failed maths test requiring a parental signature. This one was tougher: 'I've made a decision to try and find my birth mother,' I told him, twisting the cord of the phone round my finger in a nervous, sweaty twirl. 'I hope you won't mind.'

Dad quickly gave his blessing and passed the phone to Mam. I could tell from the tone of her voice that she already knew there was something afoot. This was the moment I had been dreading: telling my mother that I wished to find my other mother. I felt sick delivering the news, stumbling over the words.

There was a long pause. 'We always told you that we would support you if this day came,' Mam said eventually. 'Don't you remember how we tried to look for her when you were sixteen?'

Whenever I mention the search for my birth mother, people invariably ask the same question: 'What did your parents – your adoptive parents – think about this?'

The person sitting across from me may not mean to sound accusatory, but accusation is all I hear. I am on trial, charged with first-degree intent to disrupt domestic stability; with familial disloyalty; with turning my back on the two people who love me the most and who gave me a home when I had none. 'They were incredibly supportive,' I tell my accuser, trying to keep my irritation in check. 'They were with me one hundred per cent. I couldn't have done it without them.'

The truth is, I'm not entirely sure how my parents felt, or feel, about my decision to search for my birth mother, despite their astonishing magnanimity throughout the process. I have never had the courage to ask them directly. Once, several years ago, on a summer visit to Number 49 with my two young children, I found myself in the midst of a cataclysmic row with Mam, a shouting match unlike anything that had ever come between us before. We were squabbling about something trivial when suddenly Mam asked, 'But why did you have to search for her? Weren't we good enough?'

'Of course you were good enough – *are* good enough,' I remember pleading. 'This isn't about you. It's about me. You *must* understand that. I just needed to know where I came from. It's that simple.'

I knew that Mam understood this on some level, even if it wasn't easy for her. As she reminded me when I phoned her from Bosnia, she had offered to help me do the same thing eleven years earlier, when I was sixteen. I have a hazy memory of standing outside my parents' bedroom one afternoon, crying desolately, while Mam beseeched me to tell her what was wrong. As hard as I tried, I could not articulate the source of my pain but finally agreed that it must be connected to my adoption. That week Mam placed a call to St Patrick's Guild. 'There has been no contact from the natural mother,' Mam was told by the nun in charge. Looking back, I am grateful that the search ended there. Knowing what I know now, I don't think I would have been able, at sixteen, to handle it.

Around the same time, I developed a profound crush on a teacher at my convent school. She was tall and thin, and wore her hair short, just like me. Unlike the rest of the faculty, especially the nuns, she taught with an egalitarian and unhurried style. She conformed almost perfectly to my dream-image of my birth mother. I was lost in worship, making excuses to stay late after class and feeling my heart beating erratically whenever I saw her in the corridor. Once, in a darkened passageway that led from the basement changing rooms to the courtyard at the back of the school, I orchestrated a private meeting with this teacher at which I tried unsuccessfully to explain my jumbled thoughts. What I was trying to say was that I wished she were my birth mother. Instead, I muttered something about 'feeling lost'. The teacher was kind but firm and suggested that I confide my confusion and angst to my parents. I remember feeling mortified by her gentle rebuff and by my inability to articulate my thoughts.

Eight years later, in 1996, my mother, at my request, made a second such phone call to St Patrick's Guild. I have no recollection of what prompted this. I was twenty-four years old at the time, old enough to make the call by myself. Perhaps, as is the condition of the adopted child, I didn't feel it was my right. I was a graduate student in Boston, studying full-time while working two jobs, and I remember feeling exhausted, physically and emotionally. In early August of that year I contracted shingles and was forced to take some time off work. My birth-mother fantasy around that time centred on Mary Robinson, the campaigning lawyer who had become President of Ireland. I mined her biography, trying to work out whether she'd dropped off the radar in the winter of 1971–2; I looked for physical similarities; I saw significance in our shared passion for human rights and justice.

One afternoon, as I lay on the couch in the stifling summer heat, the mailman delivered a letter to my apartment. It was from Mam, neatly typed.

Dear Caitríona,

I hope by now your shingles have disappeared and you are a good deal stronger. You will want to be very careful of your health and try to take things a little easier. I know you have to work but rest as much as possible. You appear very run-down. Please eat well and get yourself a tonic. I enclose a copy of the letter from St Patrick's Guild. As no contact has been made since January 1973 it could take years. However if anything at all comes for you I will forward it to you without delay. I hope this does not upset you.

Lots of LOVE,
Mam and Dad

The letter from St Patrick's Guild was dated 31 July 1996 and signed by a Sister Gabriel Murphy. It was addressed to my mother.

Dear Mrs Palmer,

Further to your request by phone for background information on Caitríona. Caitríona's birth mother was, according to our records, a teacher by profession. She came from a farming background. She is described as tall with fair hair. She had a nice personality. To the best of our knowledge her father or members of her family were not aware of her pregnancy. She described Caitríona's birth father as being tall with fair reddish hair. He was working as a Building Contractor. Caitríona's birth mother's last contact with this agency was in January 1973.

I remember gulping this letter down quickly, then re-reading it slowly, trying to absorb the details on the page. It sketched only the barest details of a spectral life and yet, to me, it felt like a great revelation. I wanted to know more. But as Mam had rightly pointed out, and the letter from St Patrick's Guild confirmed, there had been no contact from my birth mother for over twenty-three years. She might be dead. She might have forgotten me. I wasn't ready to have one of those horrible possibilities confirmed, or to cope with the consequences of her being alive and willing to meet me. That night I folded the letter from St Patrick's Guild in half and put it back in the envelope.

As soon as Mam reminded me over the phone that afternoon in Bosnia about what had happened when I was sixteen, I recalled standing outside my parents' room crying for a loss that I could not articulate; at the same time I felt a rush of relief at having unburdened myself to the people I cared about the most. The worst part was over, I thought, as I placed the phone back on to the receiver and stared out of the window. With Mary and Liam on board, the search could begin.

And yet, because I was so fixated on the needs of others, I was unaware, at that moment, of the emotional precipice on which I stood. It never occurred to me that I might be wounded as a result of the search I had set in motion.

3

The plan to break into the hospital was hatched one evening around the kitchen table of the main PHR house on Pere Ćuskića, cold local beers in hand, our plates laden with meat pies and a tomato and cucumber salad prepared earlier in the day by the office housekeeper. An impressive young American journalist was with us that evening. She was visiting Tuzla to write a book on the Bosnian war and was investigating the remarkable story of Srebrenica's hospital during the three-year siege by Bosnian Serb forces. A handful of inexperienced young doctors had manned the hospital in appalling conditions during that time, performing amputations without anaesthesia or electricity, and providing patchy but heroic care for the town's 50,000 trapped men, women and children.

Around the table we listened as the journalist discussed her plans for the week, outlining a proposal to visit the hospital – which now stood abandoned – so that she could see the empty wards and corridors up close. It was an audacious idea. Srebrenica by then was under Bosnian Serb control, the entire town cleansed of all Muslim and Croat residents, and the new occupants – Bosnian Serb refugees from across the divided country – hostile to any outside interference. Getting permission from local officials to explore the hospital would be next to impossible, a colleague surmised, suggesting that the next best option was to simply let ourselves in.

PHR at that point was struggling to cope with the intense pressure to attach names to the thousands of corpses and body parts that were being extracted from the earth around eastern Bosnia. There was not enough funding to provide DNA analysis for all the exhumed remains, and so the identification process was being conducted the old-fashioned way: pairing post-mortem details with information provided by living relatives – the height of the missing person, their hair and eye colour, and whether they had any previous fractures or other distinctive bodily characteristics, like old scars or tattoos. Only when there was the strong likelihood of a positive identification would bone samples from the dead and saliva samples from a living relative be sent to the United States for full DNA analysis. The process was laborious and slow. By the winter of 1998, fewer than a hundred identifications had been made from more than 7,500 Srebrenica missing persons. It was with those grim statistics in mind that a colleague proposed that night that we join the journalist and try to get into the abandoned hospital in Srebrenica. Despite the chaos that had descended upon the hospital during the siege, she wondered aloud, might there still be medical files to be found there, containing information that could help our forensic colleagues put names to corpses?

We left Tuzla a couple of mornings later in freezing temperatures, the hills around Pere Ćuskića covered in frost, the ground crunchy beneath our feet. We travelled in a convoy of three unmarked cars, rather than the conspicuous white trucks branded with the diplomatic plates of the international protectorate overseeing the new Bosnia. In ordinary cars we would stand out less, but we knew that any new traffic to the town – particularly with Bosnian plates – might attract some unwelcome attention. One of the passengers in my car was Sabina, a Bosnian colleague who had grown up in Srebrenica and had lived in the town throughout the siege. Sabina was quiet and hard-working but her Srebrenica roots and refugee status set her apart. When she heard of our plan,

Sabina had requested to join the expedition, hoping to see the apartment – now illegally occupied by a refugee Serb family – where she had spent her childhood. Now, as our convoy made its way through the heart of Bosnian Serb territory, Sabina sat silently in the back of the car, her expression wary, the fingers of her left hand nervously twisting the gold bands she wore on her right.

For my own part, I was simply along for the ride, eager for adventure and impatient to shake off the hum of foreboding and dislocation that now followed me through every waking day in Tuzla. On the surface, I was the usual Caitríona – pleasant, productive and charming to a fault – but deep inside I felt darkly unhappy. The source of my angst was a mystery to me, so expertly hidden within the depths of my psyche that it seemed impossible to access.

We arrived in Srebrenica around mid-morning as a light snow was beginning to fall. Our little convoy crawled slowly up the steep hill of the town, the bare stalls of the makeshift market to our left, the decrepit cars of local residents parked haphazardly on the pavements to our right. On either side of the road loomed the sage and pine banks of Srebrenica's steep valley, the higher slopes covered in patchy casings of snow. The streets at first glance looked empty until we saw small groups of men huddled in doorways, some hooded and hatted against the cold. The men smoked cigarettes and watched sullenly as our convoy passed. I turned my head to watch as one man stepped into the street to spit contemptuously in our wake. 'Keep your eyes straight ahead,' urged our colleague at the wheel as he shifted gear.

The buildings on Srebrenica's streets looked half-complete. Some were missing roofs and windows, causing the December snow to gather in pillowy drifts in the corners. Others were daubed in Serb nationalist graffiti. As the road curved to the left, the Soviet-style apartment block where Sabina once lived loomed into view. Our car slowed to a crawl as she pressed her face up against the window.

The hospital stood on a hill, the lower floors obscured from view by a row of pines and a concrete wall. In the ambiguous late-morning light the building looked dreary, menacing. We drove past once, scoping out a place to park, and eventually deciding to leave our cars on a street higher up the hill where, obscured from view, we hoped they wouldn't attract too much attention. Without speaking, we walked towards the rear of the hospital, the journalist in the lead. As a colleague stood sentry at the corner of the building, the rest of us looked for the best place to gain entry. A broken window that yielded slightly when forced seemed like the easiest option. When my turn came to squeeze through the jagged edges of the window frame, the reality of what I was doing began to hit home. In my mind's eye I saw an angry mob forming. As a colleague waiting below whispered encouragement, I jumped down on to the tiled floor beneath the window, nearly slipping on a carpet of broken glass. From the cigarette butts, beer bottles and trash strewn about the floor it looked as though we weren't the first to gain entry this way. I turned back to the window to lend a hand to the next colleague struggling to climb through. Once inside we turned together towards the gloom of the murky corridors, trying to adjust our eyes to the shadowy light.

A few months later, in Dublin, I sat in the offices of St Patrick's Guild. Across the desk, dressed in a cardigan, cream blouse and navy wool skirt, sat the nun who ran the agency. Her grandmotherly grey hair was uncovered, free of the navy and white habit that had demarcated the nuns of my childhood. Two cups of tea and a plate of custard cream biscuits sat between us.

I was struggling to answer a question the nun had just posed: why now, at this stage in my life, had I decided to search for my birth mother? It felt like a trick question – what person wouldn't want to know who their mother was? – and I worried that the success of the search hung on the authenticity of my reply. I was on trial, eager to make a good impression. Weeks earlier, over the phone, the same nun had outlined the purpose of this meeting: to get my side of the story, to assess why I wanted to search and to discuss the logistics of the process. As that telephone conversation wound down there had been a vague reference to the importance of my emotional state, the need to ensure that I was of 'sound mind'. I had thought the phrase hilarious, laughing about it with friends over drinks at a bar in Sarajevo, but now I was nervously trying to project cheerful sanity. I had come to the meeting, like the good adoptee that I was, bearing flowers for the nun. But my people-pleasing skills – now in reckless overdrive – were having little obvious effect. The tea had barely been served and already I felt as though I wasn't measuring up.

I took a deep breath. What I really wanted to talk about was the way I felt as though I was unmoored: plagued by sleepless nights, anxiety and the inexplicable sensation that there was something missing in my life. I wanted to talk about Bosnia: the rotting corpses, the de-fleshing room and the irritation I felt when my forensic colleagues forgot to clean their boots and tramped mud from mass graves all over the carpet. I wanted to tell this woman about the crushing loneliness I felt every evening when I returned to my apartment and shut the door, how I missed Chris but worried that our relationship was winding down. I wanted to talk about how impotent I felt around the Srebrenica relatives and how I could offer no help other than a smile and empty reassurances in my inadequate Bosnian. I wanted to admit that living in Tuzla, surrounded by the ghosts of Srebrenica, was making me feel more than a little crazy. But I knew that such details would not demonstrate a 'sound mind'.

I remembered the previous winter's illicit stalk through the corridors of the Srebrenica hospital and the surge of delight when a colleague opened a large wooden closet in an empty room to reveal, scattered on the second shelf, a bundle of medical files. In that moment, filling our arms with the dusty paperwork, I felt a sliver of illumination. Driving back to Tuzla later that afternoon, our pilfered medical dossiers on our laps, the mood in the car jovial, I returned again to that moment, massaging the memory, trying to knead to the surface the revelation lurking beneath. What was I doing helping to search for the files of dead strangers when it was plainly obvious that I needed to hunt for my own?

I looked at the nun. 'Many times I have been asked for my medical history but have not – for obvious reasons – been able to provide it,' I ventured. 'I'd like to be able – once and for all – to gain access to my family's medical files. In case, you know, there are any serious genetic problems.' The nun nodded and made a neat note on a legal pad in front of her. Turning her gaze back towards me, she said nothing. I looked at the floor.

I tried again, this time with a hint of urgency to my voice. 'I mean, it's just important for me to know, to fill in the pieces. I've had an extremely happy life. I'm very close to my parents and very grateful, obviously, for everything that they've done for me. I'd just like to be able to meet my birth mother, to tell her how everything has turned out so well. To have a chance to say thank you.' I paused. 'Does that make sense?'

An imperceptible nod. More notations. Silence. I was aware

of a sweat stain beginning to fan out from beneath the armpits of my cotton blouse, the familiar pinprick of anxiety expanding across my belly. I hadn't expected to have to work so hard to prove my worthiness for this search. Naively, I had thought it my right.

'Of course, you are aware that there is a very extensive waiting list to join before we can activate your search request,' the nun was saying as she shifted through some paper on her desk. 'I can't say when your name is likely to come to the top of that list and of course, when it does, I must warn you that the search may not end the way you envision it. Your natural mother may no longer be alive or may not have any wish to pursue contact with you.'

'I understand, Sister,' I said obediently. 'But I'd still very much like to go ahead.'

I travelled from Bosnia to Dublin that May, wanting to prove to the nun at St Patrick's Guild that I was serious about my decision to search for my birth mother, that it was not some flighty quest. I chose the week of my niece's First Communion. Arriving at Dublin airport, I felt instant relief to be out of Tuzla and away from the dead, even if just for a week. At home, the kettle on and the house filled with the aroma of Mam's baking, it felt soothing to be back among the familiar rhythms of Number 49.

The weather that week was unusually warm and I took my parents' dog for long walks along the seafront, admiring the seagulls dipping over the grey-green waters of Sutton estuary and the purple blaze of heather on Howth Head. Sometimes Mam or Dad would see me putting the lead on the dog and say, 'Hang on, let me get my coat.' It was then – in the blustery sea air, without the awkwardness of direct eye contact – that the questions would come: 'So, how did the meeting with St Patrick's Guild go?' 'Do they have any idea when you'll come off the waiting list?' And a gentle reproach meant in the best possible way: 'You know, we don't want to upset you but you should really be prepared for all eventualities. She might even be dead.'

It was easier to discuss the topic with my childhood friends, an eclectic and loyal bunch of pals. These were the people I'd spent endless hours with as a teenager, hanging out on a low-slung wall in a nearby housing estate, all paisley shirts, black kohl eyeliner, Doc Marten boots and bad eighties hair. A mixed group – the boys went to the local St Paul's secondary school, the girls to the convent-run Manor House – we had all fallen for one another at some point. It was within this group that I had my first drink, my first drag on a joint, my first real French kiss. Many of these friends had remained in Dublin and it was to them that I turned that week at home, filling them in on my decision to search for my birth mother over pints of Smithwick's and Guinness in the pub just round the corner from Number 49.

At the end of that week I returned to St Patrick's Guild to meet with the social worker now assigned to my case, a woman named Catherine who exuded warmth and practicality. Catherine was the consummate professional, but I could see promising flickers of enthusiasm, humour and compassion. Unlike the nun that oversaw the Guild's adoption reunions, Catherine did not put me on the defensive, and I felt at ease in her company. On the train home I allowed myself – for the first time – to feel excitement about the impending search. Finally, it was about to happen.

Back at home that night, I sat down to record an account of the meeting in my diary, flicking back a few pages to read an entry from the previous month, the night before my twenty-seventh birthday.

Tomorrow, as always, will be reserved for my birth mother – wherever she is. Perhaps, though, this will be the last birthday where I will feel sadness and concern for her happiness. It's hard to believe that a search of sorts will begin soon. I don't think I realize the impact that this will have on my life. Whatever your name is – if you are out there – please think of me tomorrow as I will of you. Perhaps we'll meet each other soon.

Five weeks later, back in Bosnia, I received a call from Catherine to say that my name had moved to the top of the waiting list and that my search was now active. I was shocked by the speed of the process, filled with a sudden buyer's remorse and a sense that things were moving too quickly. The jaunty feeling that had followed me back to Bosnia after my meeting with Catherine quickly dissipated, replaced by an odd sensation of foreboding and unease. I felt conflicted. I wanted the train to stop, at least temporarily, so I could catch my breath. 'I'll need you to fax me a list of questions for your tracing request,' Catherine told me, explaining that these would be the first words my birth mother would hear from me once she had been found. I made some quick notes on a yellow legal pad as possible questions formed in my mind. *Where does she live? Is she married? How many kids does she have? Who is my biological father? Is she happy? Can you tell her that I've had a wonderful life?*

That night, a gin and tonic by my side and a pillow at my back, I sat on the carpeted floor of the balcony overlooking the garden of my house in Pere Ćuskića. I had taken to spending the warmer evenings here, watching the kids playing soccer on the dusty street below and enjoying the hazy pink sunsets behind the hills to the west. My housemate, Margaret, had left Bosnia some months before and, although I missed her, I was grateful for these quiet moments alone. I badly needed time to think. The decision to search was mine alone: all I had to do was fax Catherine the list of tracing questions. Did I want this to happen? After all my talk and years of wondering, was I really ready to let my birth mother into my life?

On the carpet next to me lay my diary, a beautiful hand-crafted leather tome that my friend Edward had picked up as a gift on a recent trip to Venice. Never a prodigious journal-keeper, I was now making regular entries. I opened the diary and turned to a new page. At the top, in capital letters, I wrote, 'What do I want?' Underneath, beginning with number one, I began to list:

1. *Peace of mind*
2. *Erasing that awful feeling of mourning that dogs me like a shadow*
3. *Resolution*
4. *A rest*
5. *My mother's love*

Turning to the next page, I paused and then continued.

I want, want, want this to work. I want this to work more than I've wanted anything else. I want to know what happened and what gave her the courage to do what she did. I want to be her friend, and for her to be mine. I simply want to know her name.

It was clear now what my decision would be. I put the diary down and walked barefoot inside to the apartment, where my laptop sat on the dining-room table. I opened it up and began to type a list of tracing questions. It was 6 July 1999. Tomorrow the search would begin.

Two weeks later, the search officially underway, I left Bosnia for a long weekend, flying to Paris to see Chris, who had moved there temporarily for work. After a long separation, our relationship was on shaky ground. I was reluctant to move to Paris. Chris, forever patient, had suggested London. Again, I demurred.

At Charles de Gaulle airport, Chris was waiting at the arrivals barrier, arms outstretched. We took a cab to the east of Paris, where he now lived in a bright studio apartment with an enormous walled patio that overlooked the city skyline. We were tentative with each other at first, shy after so many months apart.

On the Sunday morning we slept in late, heading out after noon to visit the Père Lachaise Cemetery, walking hand in hand amid the crypts and vaults of the former Jesuit retreat. In the scorching heat I became quickly dehydrated. At a *tabac* near the cemetery Chris stopped to buy some water while I waited outside beneath a shaded awning next to the newsstands. The front pages of several newspapers caught my eye: John F. Kennedy Jr, his wife, Carolyn Bessette, and her sister Lauren had been lost when their small plane crashed into the sea off Martha's Vineyard. Chris bought one of the papers and we took it to a shady spot to read. The news stayed with us for the rest of the day, and later that night, beneath the stained-glass atrium of the Brasserie Bofinger in the fourth arrondissement, we continued to talk about the crash. Ruminating on the Kennedys allowed us to avoid an uncomfortable topic that shadowed us throughout the weekend: our own uncertain future. It was clear that despite the Paris sunshine and our tenderness towards one another, our future looked increasingly bleak. As we moved through the city I saw snatches of the old us, so full of love and good intentions for the life that we could lead. But I was distracted and anxious, dogged by uncertainty and ambivalence. The search for my birth mother had begun only two weeks previously but I was already feeling frustrated. All of this, while sitting in the sunshine on Chris's balcony, I recorded in my diary:

Still no news. I'm trying to remain nonchalant and calm, but the lack of news is bothering me greatly. Perhaps she really, truly is dead and St Patrick's Guild is contemplating the next awful move? Every time the damn mobile rings I think it is the social worker with news. I'm sure the call – when it does come – will be at the most inappropriate time.

The entries ended with a plea to my nameless maternal ghost:

Please. Wherever you are, just take the courage to go ahead with this. It means so, so much to me. Please.

On 20 July I returned to Sarajevo, happy to be back once again among the familiar minarets and terracotta tiles of the Ottoman city. Scheming to delay my return to Tuzla for as long as possible, I arranged meetings in PHR's Sarajevo headquarters, a modern building nicknamed the 'White House' that stood on a hill close to the cobblestoned old town, Baščaršija. I loved working out of this office, strolling down to the old town at lunchtime with friends to eat at a restaurant near a whitewashed mosque that served bowls of fragrant lamb stew with fluffy rice. At night I bunked down at one of PHR's staff houses close to the office, an apartment inhabited by my colleagues Heather and Rick, American anthropologists. Over the previous six months Heather and I had grown close, bonding over relationship woes and office gossip. The friendship had begun the previous December, during my first-ever mass-grave exhumation near the Bosnian Serb town of Sanski Most. In a wooded area, high on a hill, Heather and Rick had abseiled into an underground cave

43

where the skeletal remains of 124 civilians had lain in a jumbled mess since the early days of the war. I stayed above ground, peering into the hole and reporting back to headquarters as the body count rose. Next to me stood an agitated Bosnian official, an older man who had spent time as a prisoner in the same Serb concentration camp where the victims below had lived out their final days. He demanded my constant attention, pulling up his shirt to show me his white belly covered in livid purple scars, received during lengthy torture sessions at the camp. Back at our depressing Soviet-style hotel in the evenings, the furnishings all orange polyester, Heather would tease me for my polite indulgence of the Bosnian official, who by then was following me around mournfully, treating me as his therapist.

It was Heather who I was laughing with on 26 July, the last day of the Sarajevo sojourn, as I sat in the White House waiting for my boss, Laurie, to get off the phone. We were sitting on swivel chairs in the main office of the building, a room with multiple desks where PHR's forensic scientists came to write up their exhumation reports. Heather was mid report, bored and eager to procrastinate. Outside, Laurie's white jeep was packed and ready for the three-hour drive to Tuzla. Laurie's call dragged on and I decided to wait in the sunshine of the courtyard below. As I stepped outside, waving in response to the friendly shopkeeper across the street, my mobile phone rang. It was Laurie, I assumed, off the phone and wondering where I had gone. I picked it up to hear a familiar Irish accent.

'Hi, Caitríona, this is Catherine. Are you sitting down? I have some big news.'

The news was good: Catherine had just spoken directly with my birth mother. Her name was Sarah. She was married, had three children and lived in greater Dublin. She had, in her own words, been waiting for this moment for twenty-seven years.

'She's away on holidays right now,' Catherine told me. 'As soon as she's back in Dublin, she's going to come in to meet me and I'll get a bigger picture then. But she wanted me to tell you that she sends you her love and that she has thought of you always.'

By the time Laurie emerged from the White House I was sitting on the front steps of the building, mute, staring off into space. The details of my birth mother's life were minimal – name, marital status, number of kids – but my brain was struggling to absorb them. Above all, I was struggling to take in the electrifying idea that she was *alive*, that I was now privy to direct communications from her: *she sends you her love; she has thought of you always; she has been waiting for this moment for the past twenty-seven years.*

'Are you OK?' Laurie asked, glancing with concern in my direction as she threw a duffel bag on to the back seat of the jeep.

'I'm not sure,' I said, getting to my feet and opening the passenger door to climb inside. 'Long story. I'll tell you in the car as we drive.'

By the time we reached Tuzla that night, I was emotionally drained and desperate to be alone. It had felt good to recount the news to Laurie; the mere act of speaking Sarah's name made her seem more real. But I craved my own company and the chance to process events. At Pere Ćuskića I helped Laurie unload the car and then said goodnight, waving at the local kids as I made my way inside. I had a strong urge to call Chris but knew that he was travelling on business and unreachable. Instead I poured myself a drink and opened my bag to find my diary. In the car my mood had been erratic:

ebullient one moment, thoughtful and withdrawn the next. By the time I opened a fresh page, writing the date, 26 July, on the top right-hand corner, I was feeling buoyant once again. I began to write.

A momentous day. The day my mother finally reached out and found me. The day she heard my name for the first time. The day I heard hers. The day we finally acknowledged the ghosts of the past and grasped the potential of the future . . . I am nurturing an odd but wonderful feeling since getting the news this afternoon. It's hard to describe but I feel as though I have acquired a new part, an additional piece of me that sits snugly inside me somewhere, glowing, warming me, helping me. I simply have to whisper her name – Sarah – and feel its glow . . . Today, for the first time ever, I did not have to imagine where or what my mother was doing. Today I actually knew. She is on holiday with her family. She can't wait to get to Dublin to meet with Catherine. She sends me her love. Next birthday I will not have to imagine where she is or what she's doing. For the first time I'll actually know . . .

I spent the following week obsessively waiting for Catherine to call again, wildly grasping for my mobile phone every time it rang. The nameless preoccupation that had followed me over the past eighteen months had evaporated, replaced by an irrepressible surge in confidence. I was indefatigable, walking on air, and probably – although my colleagues were too kind to say so – more than a little irritating. On my desk lay an article about PHR's exhumation process that I was drafting for a major medical journal, but I struggled to muster any enthusiasm for the task. I spent hours picking distractedly at my keyboard and staring out of my office window, daydreaming and unreachable, in a constant state of speculation, wondering what Sarah was doing, whether she had left her vacation spot and returned to Dublin.

Chris was in Sarajevo on business the following week, and I went there to join him. That Friday we jumped in a car and drove spontaneously to Split, a Roman limestone city on the Dalmatian coast, then boarded a ferry bound for the island of Brač. For two nights we stayed in a little pension near a rocky beach, sleeping in a four-poster bed that the owners claimed was once used by the Archduke Franz Ferdinand. In the morning we sat on the balcony overlooking the Adriatic and ate homemade fig jam, cheese and crusty bread. It should have been idyllic, but I spent all weekend looking for ways to pick a fight. We returned to Sarajevo the following Monday morning uncoupled and heartbroken.

A few days later I was in the morgue in Tuzla, sitting around a long table with Laurie and the chief pathologist discussing the Srebrenica identification strategy for the rest of the year. I had switched off my mobile phone before entering the morgue, preferring to risk having Catherine's call go to voicemail than to play out such an intensely personal moment in front of my colleagues. After the meeting ended I stepped outside into the car park to check voicemail. Sure enough, there was a message from Catherine: Sarah had come to St Patrick's Guild earlier that morning. Could I call her back before 5 p.m. Irish time?

I called Catherine later that afternoon from Laurie's office, a narrow perch on the floor above the main operations room, and the only room in the building with a landline that could make international calls. In an adjoining office, just outside, sat our sleepy administrative manager, who handed me a telephone log without looking up. I briefly hesitated, wanting to tell him what the call was about, but quickly decided against it. Once inside, feeling nauseated with excitement, I sat in Laurie's enormous black swivel chair and closed my eyes. As the line echoed with the familiar cheery *brring-brring* of an Irish landline, I realized that I had forgotten to bring my notebook. Looking around the office, I spotted Laurie's portable desk printer and grabbed a white page of A4 paper from the printer tray.

That piece of paper sits before me now, faded and creased after fifteen years of safekeeping within my diary. No matter where my immigrant odyssey has taken me – The Hague, London, Tehran, Washington – this scrap of paper has followed, tucked within the folds of my diary, safe from my children's nimble and prowling fingers. It is as precious to me as a holy relic. Holding it in my hands, I can still taste the exhilaration that coursed through me that afternoon as Catherine came on the line. 'Well, Sarah was here today and met with me for over an hour,' she said. 'I've so much to tell you.' Looking at the paper now, the notes that I scribbled that afternoon almost jump off the page.

Very excited, nervous. Very happy. The first words on the page, scrawled across the top left-hand corner, a direct quote from Sarah in response to the news that I had sought her out. Further to the left are three circles, one on top of the other. In each of the circles sits a number, the last two blackened out. Only the first circle is legible, *48*: Sarah's age. *No health issues. Three children.* To the right of this, one on top of the other, I list the names of her children in birth order. *Padraig, Siobhán, John.* In heavy pen I've underlined the name of Padraig, I'm not sure why. *Husband – Michael. Living and working in Dublin. From a farm background. Off for summer* – a reference to her job as a schoolteacher – *dividing her time between . . .* the sentence trails off. And then a line that I will obsess over in the coming weeks, Sarah's reflection on having me back in her life: *She feels that part of her is complete.*

Growing up, my birth mother was the star of my adoptee fantasies. There seemed to be no space in my imagination for the other person who had given me life, my birth father. At times it felt as though I was the product of a peculiar Irish immaculate conception. Insofar as my birth father figured in my fantasies, his role was purely functional, as a supporting actor in the movie starring my mother. Like any Hollywood heartthrob, he was broad-shouldered, handsome and charming. His manners were impeccable. He was clearly in love with my mother and focused most of his attention on her. In these fantasies, he and I barely interacted, our mutual attention directed towards my mother, the undisputed star of the show. We orbited around her, awestruck, captivated, desperate for her love.

Even as I became an adult, and developed a more realistic sense of the sorts of circumstances that had probably led to my being given up for adoption, my childhood fantasies of my birth parents remained very much alive. But now, over the phone, Catherine was puncturing the fantasy. *Hasn't been in contact w/ my father. Details haven't been correct – were in a relationship – didn't last – he had been in another long-term relationship – married the other person. Hasn't seen or spoken to him in a long time.* Beneath this paragraph I noted and underlined the location on Ireland's west coast where my biological father was born. Next to it are two words: *would talk*. I have no idea what that means. Underneath is another sentence, again underlined: *Dad is a doctor*. This is a reference not to my biological father but to Sarah's belief that I was adopted into the family of a respectable middle-class Dublin doctor. This, I surmised, was a fib told by St Patrick's Guild, on the theory that it would somehow make her feel better about her loss.

On the right-hand side of the page, beneath the scribbled names of my half-siblings, I drew a rectangular box. Jotted inside is Catherine's suggestion for the next step in the process: *write to her*. Next to this I write and then subsequently

49

black out in broad strokes: *include a photograph*. Near the top of the page, beneath the proclamation that Sarah is *very happy*, lurks the first hint that all might not be so well. Two fragmentary sentences: *One concern – family doesn't know/husband doesn't know. Didn't say at the time.*

Behind my search for Sarah lurked two consistent fears: that she might be dead or – worse – that she might be unwilling to hear from me. Both of those fears had proved unfounded. But the possibility that Sarah had kept my identity a secret had never once crossed my mind. My adoptee daydreams had featured not just a birth mother, but an entire extended family – grandparents, aunts and uncles – mourning my loss. Was it possible that, in the minds of Sarah's family, I didn't actually exist?

That night, sitting on the balcony overlooking Pere Ćuskića, I felt bizarrely deflated. My mind could not move past the fact that Sarah had kept my existence a secret for so long. Did my wish to establish contact with my birth mother – to unearth my identity – override the rights and needs of an innocent family that I did not know? Was I being selfish? Was there room in Sarah's life for us all?

Squinting in the waning evening light, I glanced down at my mobile phone to see whether it was too late in Paris to call Chris. Reflexively I began to dial his number before realizing with a jolt that that door was now shut. Instead I stood up and went back inside the apartment. In the absence of my best friend my diary would have to do.

Sarah met with St Patrick's Guild today . . . The news was wonderful but I feel slightly deflated. This is due to the discovery that Sarah has not told her husband, her family, or indeed her children of my existence. I cannot believe that she has carried this burden alone for so long and feel remarkably angry and frustrated at a society that fostered such silence in those it deemed immoral. How she could have stayed silent for so long amazes me. I am now so fearful for the consequences that I am about to [inflict] on her family and husband and cannot imagine that I may bring strain and strife into the lives of people that I don't know, but whose acceptance I crave. Basically I am afraid. Afraid for Sarah, afraid for her husband and children, and afraid for myself that I may be disappointed in the end.

4

Dear Sarah,

You cannot imagine the hundreds of letters that I have composed to you in my head during the past two decades. To finally have an opportunity to write to you in person, and know that you will read this letter, is a joy and honour that is difficult to describe.

I still find it excruciating to reread the first letter that I wrote to Sarah in the early autumn of 1999. I lost the original document years ago, buried somewhere in a desktop folder on the laptop that was my workhorse at PHR. Over a decade later, during a brief visit to Dublin, I tentatively asked Sarah whether she had saved any of the letters that I had sent to her over the years. I was shy about this request, fearful about upsetting Sarah. I knew too that there was a strong likelihood that Sarah had destroyed my correspondence. An image of her feeding a fire with my letters and postcards swam into view. But in the end, my curiosity won out: I felt like an archaeologist scrabbling through the dirt, hunting for artefacts.

'I have them all hidden at home, Caitríona,' Sarah told me that day. 'I can dig them out. Would you like me to photocopy them and send them to you?'

I heard nothing more until a couple of weeks later when, back in Washington following my trip to Ireland, a large brown envelope arrived in the mail, Sarah's familiar cursive scrawled across the front. Inside were cards, letters, postcards that I had sent from all the places – Holland, London, Iran and Washington, DC – where I had lived since leaving Bosnia. As far as I could tell, she had kept everything I'd sent her. Enclosed was a handwritten note:

Caitríona, Hope this arrives safely. If not I can photocopy again. Say a big hi to all,

Lots of love, Sarah xxxxx

At the top of the pile was my first letter to Sarah, dated 1 October 1999. Looking back, I realize that it took me seven weeks to write to her: a delay that now seems incomprehensible, given how much I had agonized over the single week that it took Sarah to return Catherine's phone call. The letter was typed, and I had used a font designed to look like handwriting. I wanted my first letter to Sarah to be perfect – I wanted Caitríona Palmer to *appear* perfect – and so, rather than write quickly and freely, I drafted and redrafted, procrastinated and dawdled.

It is an endurance test to read that letter through to the end. The persona of the writer seems so contrived, so saccharine and obsequious; it is painful to acknowledge that it is me. The prose is peppered with schmaltzy declarations and exclamation marks. I come across as pretentious and false.

My current work in Bosnia, where I come in daily contact with people forced from their homes by ethnic cleansing, has made me realize that my complaints of giving up the luxury of life in Boston were unjustified. Working with grief-stricken refugees and a mountain of dead bodies certainly puts perspective on one's life.

Reading this letter fifteen years on, I feel sorry for my insecure younger self, for the person who strained to demonstrate to

Sarah that she was not your average twenty-seven-year-old from north Dublin, that she was special. I also recognize the little child seeking approval from the mythical birth mother of her dreams. The letter, for all its wordiness, amounts to a single simple petition: Please like me.

I must first thank you from the bottom of my heart for your positive and happy reaction to Catherine's phone call. Knowing the shock you must have felt, I was so relieved to hear from Catherine that you were pleased at my wish to make contact. Your positive reaction filled me with a sense of happiness and fulfilment that has not left me since that fateful Monday afternoon in Sarajevo when Catherine told me that she had spoken with you. To simply know that you are alive and well was news enough, but to learn that you were keen to make contact with me was something I very much hoped for. Thank you once again.

It was wonderful once more to speak with Catherine following your meeting with her in Dublin and to learn more details of your life, family and self. Following these many years of knowing very little about you, these new facts and figures read like volumes of history. I am so happy to know that you are married with three wonderful children. They must be such a comfort and joy to you and I'm sure you're very proud of them. I look forward to hearing more about them and your husband at your leisure.

It's very difficult to know where to begin this letter. In fact I must confess that this must be the twentieth draft! There is simply so much to say; so many stories to tell and so many characters to introduce. Although the temptation is to cram the last twenty-seven years into this one letter, I'd like to take this letter to tell you a little bit about myself – where I am now, how I got here, where I hope to go to. I hope that the weeks, months and years that lie ahead will give us both the opportunity to catch up on one another's lives and to fill in the many missing gaps.

It takes four pages before I summon up the courage to mention my parents. Already I can sense the tension in my writing. I am hanging back, afraid of hurting Sarah's feelings. But there is so much of me that I have absorbed from Mary Palmer, so many of her traits that have become my own. And so, addressing the elephant in the room, I tell Sarah about 'Mam'.

She is incredibly smart, perceptive and funny. She is also exceptionally loving and kind and perhaps the most generous person I know . . . She unabashedly showers me with love and affection and has been my biggest supporter throughout my decision to search for you.

I introduce my dad as

my life mentor and closest friend. I would like to think we are very alike – a product of nurture versus nature – but I realize that I am nowhere near as good a person as he . . . he is quiet, gentle, intellectual and unassuming. Everybody who knows him refers to him as a saint, and in many ways he is. He raised all three of us not to talk ill of people and to constantly see the good in others . . . he is beloved by everybody who meets him.

I try to make Sarah feel better about her loss, to suggest that she did the right thing by giving me up. I have the temerity, like a US president addressing the troops, to thank Sarah for her service, to suggest that the entire Palmer clan has been enriched by her sacrifice. I am a journalist hustling a story with a pre-determined hook: that my adoption was the best thing that could ever have happened to me, that I am a far happier person as a result.

I cannot tell you how fortunate I am to have been adopted into such a wonderful family. I have you to thank for this. My only regret is that you were not aware of my happiness and contentment throughout all these years. I regret too that you were not aware that the huge sacrifice that you made was very much appreciated not only by me, but by my entire family . . . I am aware that you must have thought of me during this time and wondered whether you did the right thing. I simply want to tell you that yes, you did. I am so happy with life and with myself, and so grateful to you and to my parents for making me the person that I am today.

I tell Sarah a lie: that I went in search of her in order to thank her. I don't write about the insomniac nights spent wandering my apartment in Boston, the inexplicable rages that sometimes welled up from deep within and the fact that I have lived an entire life without ever feeling complete.

The decision to search for you came relatively easy, although it took many years to work up the courage to do so. I was lucky in having my folks and family to support me. My main motivation in contacting you is simply to say 'Thank you' . . .

I give her a history lecture: citing the injustices visited by Church, state and society upon Sarah and tens of thousands of other unmarried Irish mothers who were shunned and institutionalized; compressing Sarah's lived experience into a neat historical narrative.

I cannot imagine the agony you must have felt in reaching the decision to put me up for adoption and I admire you so much for doing so. Ireland in 1972 was hardly a benevolent society for unmarried mothers and I cannot imagine the pressure and pain you must have felt. I am so sorry that you had to undergo this pain alone and carry this burden unshared for so long. I have spent much time thinking about this and have nothing but the deepest admiration and respect for you.

I wonder whether I could have shown such similar courage. You must be a remarkable person.

On the last page, I acknowledge to Sarah that I know she has kept my existence a secret.

I very much hope, Sarah, to meet you sometime in the not too distant future . . . I am, however, very aware that your husband and family do not know of my existence so I would urge you to consider pursuing this relationship, or meeting me, only when you feel most comfortable to do so.

And then, in a gesture that I will later deeply regret, I offer the first of repeated assurances that my patience – my tolerance for being kept a secret – is endless.

Please take all the time you need. There is no rush whatsoever – I will happily wait for as long as you'd like. It really is my pleasure to do so.

On the evening of 21 December 1999 I took an overnight bus from Sarajevo to Zagreb. The snow was nearly three feet deep as the bus pulled out of the terminus, the result of a massive storm that had closed Sarajevo airport. I had a one-way ticket for a flight from Zagreb to London the following day, and the eight-hour bus ride north was my only hope of getting out. I had made plans to spend the holidays with my family in Dublin, reconnecting with my brother, David, and his girlfriend, Jo, who would be coming from London. But there was a more urgent reason for me to get to Dublin: on 23 December, I was to meet Sarah for the first time at the St Patrick's Guild offices on Haddington Road.

Beneath the floor of the bus, in the freezing luggage hold, sat a large suitcase and a black duffel bag, both bursting at the seams. My life in Bosnia had come to a close. Three weeks earlier, following months of a protracted and nasty turf war, PHR had pulled the plug on our programmes across Bosnia. Now, under an unhappy rearrangement that felt like a coup, control of the identification and exhumation projects would pass to another, much larger organization and I was out of a job.

Twenty-four hours later I was back home in a festively decked-out Number 49 and having an anxiety attack over an innocuous bouquet of flowers. The flowers in question – a mixture of roses, carnations and delphiniums, wrapped in cellophane and tied together with a nylon red bow – were intended as a gift to Sarah the following morning. But they were gaudy, and I hated the sight of them. I wanted something more ethereal: simple, white, sophisticated, timeless. But with less than fourteen hours between my arrival in Dublin and the meeting with Sarah the following day, I had taken Liam and Mary up on their offer to order flowers from their usual florist, a family business that doubled as a funeral home. That night I pouted and fretted over the flowers. I knew, deep down, that my tantrum masked a more terrifying reality. As I sat on my childhood bed, my diary in my lap, my bedside clock showing that I had less than ten hours left before meeting Sarah, I understood – for the first time – that I was beginning to have second thoughts.

I am feeling as though I have begun a journey that is impossible to reverse . . . I worry that I won't act appropriately, that Sarah will cry and I won't. Or that after the many months of heartache, angst, anger – the closure of PHR, the grief of the Srebrenica families that I befriended – that I will cry not just for Sarah but for the loss that I've seen and endured this past year.

The following morning, I did not cry, even after Sarah rushed towards me – a blur of blonde hair, bangles and imitation fur – and held me close, repeating my name over and over and over in raspy, gentle sobs. I stood there in shock, holding this quivering stranger in my arms, wishing that she would let me go, aghast at how utterly empty I felt. Closing my eyes, still caught in her grip, I can remember literally – in the still of my mind – willing myself to cry. But no tears came. Instead, I stood there, soothing Sarah, patting her on the back and marvelling at both the intensity of her keening and the well of nothingness inside me. As the embrace endured, I was afraid to be the first to pull away, and wished that Sarah would let me go. Suddenly the whole thing seemed a terrible mistake.

I remain haunted by that first meeting, playing the scene over and over again in my mind, wishing that I could have acted differently, ashamed that my emotions failed so spectacularly to rise to the occasion. The books on adoption reunions that I have read over the years assure me that my reaction was normal, that reuniting with a birth parent is often so overwhelming that our senses shut down entirely. But I find little solace in this. My detachment and composure that day bother me still. I was the one who had sought Sarah out, who had started us both on this road. Why, now, did I feel nothing other than clinical, dispassionate ambivalence?

I can remember still, with great clarity, the terror of waiting for Sarah to arrive that day – the ebb and flow of nausea, scanning the room for a wastebasket in case my stomach failed me, the sound of Sarah's footsteps as she approached the door. I remember too the intensity of our embrace, the cloying scent of her perfume, the softness of her velvety cheek, the scratchiness of her fake fur against my face. My first impression was that the coat made her look cheap – nothing like the beautiful goddess who had dominated my child-hood dreams. (Sarah would later tell me that she dressed in this way thinking I would find her more attractive, youth-ful.) I hugged her back, smiled and soothed her tears. Weirdly, as I held her trembling frame, I felt like the parent, the protector, in the room.

I remember too feeling alarmed some moments later when, satisfied that all was proceeding to plan, Catherine announced that she was briefly stepping out to allow us some time to chat in private. I suddenly panicked. I would be alone with Sarah. An irrational thought flitted across my mind: that Sarah might try to kidnap me. I wanted to tell Catherine that I'd be much happier if she stayed, but I lacked the courage to speak my mind. Instead I smiled my acquiescence and watched with apprehension as she left the room.

I have very little recollection of what Sarah and I spoke about when we were alone, but I do remember clearly that she quickly grew fidgety and, all of a sudden, suggested that we leave.

'How are you getting home?' she asked. 'Can I give you a lift?'

I did not know how to respond. Catherine had not yet reappeared and it was my understanding that she would have to wrap up the meeting before we left. I had also not antici-pated that Sarah and I might leave together – something I certainly didn't want to do. But Sarah seemed determined, gathering up her coat and reaching across the coffee table to grab the garish bouquet. 'Let's head out,' she said. 'I can drop you home. My car is right outside.'

We made our way down the narrow hallway towards the dark stairwell. My fear was coming true: my own mother was kidnapping me. I felt voiceless, vulnerable, six years old all over again. This was not working out the way I had imagined.

I wanted to stay and debrief with Catherine, to get her thoughts on how it had all gone, to ask whether the detachment I felt was normal or whether, as I suspected, I was some sort of freak. I also desperately wanted time alone, before returning to Number 49, to process the events that had just occurred. Was Sarah actually suggesting that she drive me home to Raheny and drop me outside the house? Would I have to invite her inside?

Catherine's head appeared round a door at the end of the hallway. She seemed startled to see us, coats on, heading down the stairs. With my eyes I beseeched her to intervene. She followed us down the stairs, Sarah now heading straight for the large wooden front door.

'Are you finished already?' I heard Catherine say. 'Why don't you come back upstairs so we can chat about how things went?'

But Sarah was now at the door, her long slender fingers turning the brass latch to the left, a sliver of light from the open door casting a narrow shadow on the wall behind.

'No, I'm dropping Caitríona home,' she said, turning to face Catherine with a smile but also with a quiet defiance that I have never seen her exhibit since. 'Isn't that right?' Sarah said, looking at me.

I felt caught in the headlights. Catherine looked perplexed, even angry, although I knew it was not directed at me. I understood that we were breaking all the rules on adoption reunions, that this was bad manners. It was not how I had been raised, to rush away without properly acknowledging our host. I desperately wanted the courage to tell Sarah to head along herself, that I would see her soon. But it seemed I was unable to defy my birth mother within an hour of meeting her for the first time, and so, looking directly at Catherine, I mustered up a smile. 'It's fine,' I told her. 'Totally fine.'

Catherine's puzzled face was the last thing I saw before the large wooden door of St Patrick's Guild clicked softly behind our backs. Sarah was already two steps ahead, rummaging in her bag for her keys, making her way towards her car. It was raining hard now and the December dampness made me shiver as I walked down the granite steps. I pulled my black fitted jacket tighter across my chest and followed dutifully in her wake.

An hour later I was walking up the short concrete driveway towards the frosted-glass front door of Number 49. I had never been so happy to see the privet hedges and pebble-dashed exteriors of the houses in the estate. I felt numb, unmoored from my body, adrift in a haze of shock and regret. In my mind everything had gone wrong – everything about Sarah was wrong – and I was full of remorse at having brought this fragile creature into my life.

The drive across the city with Sarah had been strained and tense: she was a distracted driver, slow to respond to traffic signals, sometimes veering into the nearside lane. The interior of her car smelt of wet dog and looked a mess – something she apologized for incessantly. While we made small talk, I made discreet attempts to flick away the coarse dog hairs that now flecked my trousers. Finally we reached Clontarf Road station, from where a train would take me the final three stops to Raheny. I had insisted, politely, that we do it this way, terrified at the awkwardness that might ensue from an impromptu drop-off outside Number 49. We sat for a short time chatting in her car, the rain now coming down in torrents, the signal from Sarah's hazard lights making a soothing *tick-tock* sound in the interior. We hugged briefly, the embrace somehow less jarring than the first, and agreed we would meet again, with Catherine's help, in the New Year. I stood in the rain and waved politely as Sarah drove away. I wondered, as I watched her car disappear into the low winter light, what lie Sarah had told her husband that morning.

Now, letting myself in to Number 49, I steeled myself. Through the glass doors I could see Liam and Mary drinking tea at the kitchen table. My heart sank when I saw their expectant faces. I was emotionally drained, irritated by the sight of them, overwhelmed at the prospect of a parental post-mortem.

'How did it go?' asked Mam, getting up when she saw me to put a fresh kettle of water on the boil. 'Sit down, love, will you have a cup of tea? You must be frozen.'

'It went really well,' I lied, avoiding any eye contact. 'She's wonderful, really lovely.' I took off my black jacket and placed it across the back of my usual chair beneath the framed picture of the Sacred Heart. 'The whole thing couldn't have gone better.'

I spun the same lie the following evening at the Cedar Lounge during the annual Christmas Eve reunion with my school friends. The mood in the pub was loud and festive and I was happy to be back among my mates, relieved to have the meeting with Sarah behind me and eager to down the pints of beer that flowed in an endless procession. After a few drinks I began to enjoy the excitement that my reunion with Sarah was generating, revelling in the amazement of my friends who asked variations on the same few questions: Does she look like you? Did you cry when you met her? What did your parents say? When will you see her again?

It would, in fact, be another two weeks before Sarah and I met again. In the meantime, five days after Christmas, I caught a flight to Edinburgh, part of a large group of friends from Bosnia – journalists, diplomats, human-rights specialists – who had planned to ring in the millennium Hogmanay at our friend David's ancestral home, a beautiful manse set on hundreds of Highland forested acres. At Edinburgh airport, I collected my bags and sat in the arrivals hall with a coffee and a copy of the *Guardian* to await an incoming flight from London. On board was my new boyfriend, Dan De Luce, a thirty-four-year-old American journalist. I'd first met Dan on a hot day in 1997, my first summer in Sarajevo. Dan, who had spent the previous five years covering the war in the former Yugoslavia, was Reuters's Sarajevo bureau chief, and it was Chris – aware that I would be living in a city with no friends – who knew him through work and suggested that I look him up. Dan was over an hour late for that first meeting, arriving, in no apparent hurry, his hands slung into the pockets of his jeans, at the cafe opposite the Catholic cathedral where I sat pretending to read a newspaper. We hit it off immediately, agreeing to meet up for dinner the following night with another American journalist who Dan thought might also be able to help me find my way.

The following night I arrived at the Reuters office to find an apologetic Dan, late again, on deadline frantically filing a breaking story. Dinner would have to wait. I passed the time chatting to the night watchman overseeing the property, a gentle man with lively eyes named Hiro. An hour later, Dan's story dispatched to London, we finally left, heading out into the warm night to a cosy restaurant down the cobblestoned hill. Passing the Reuters office on his way home hours later, Dan bumped into Hiro as he was making his final nightly checks. Hiro seemed excited to see him: 'Mr Dan, that woman who was here tonight, the woman from Ireland? You will marry her. I tell you, you will marry her.'

It was hard to ignore the attraction that pulsed between Dan and me in the summer of 1997, but because of my relationship with Chris there was no possibility of a romance.

Instead we became friends, meeting up occasionally for coffee or dinner, and dancing together some weekend nights at 'the Bar', Sarajevo's hippest post-war drinking hole, a basement room with a live DJ and a raised dance floor. I flirted with Dan, daydreamed about him and tried to keep a careful distance, but there were a few close calls. Once, very late at night in December 1997, Dan dropped by my apartment in Sarajevo to borrow a black duffel bag for his flight back home to California the next day. I ran down the stairwell to let him in, leading the way as we climbed back towards my open apartment door. Halfway up, the stairwell lights – operated by a timer – flicked off, plunging us into sudden darkness. I turned round, feeling out blindly in the dark for the light switch but finding Dan's outstretched arm. We stood together in the shadows, my right arm resting gently on his, the air around us expanding with silence and anticipation. I felt myself melting into the floor with longing and desire, wishing, wishing, that he would bend to kiss me. Finally the light came back on and we pulled away, sheepish and embarrassed. But for months the intensity of that moment lingered in my mind.

It was Dan's hand that I held as I climbed the granite steps of Haddington Road in early January 2000, moments away from meeting Sarah for the second time. The previous day Dan and I had flown back to Dublin following the Hogmanay celebrations, and we were planning a four-day sightseeing trip around Ireland. Ten weeks earlier, and two years after our moment on the stairwell, he and I had kissed for the first time in my apartment in Tuzla, awakening in each of us a sense of homecoming and belonging so profound that we knew immediately that our mutual search for a life partner was over. By the time I left Bosnia for Dublin two months later we were already talking marriage. Dan's trip to Dublin would be the first step in our orchestrated campaign to 'meet the parents'. Sarah was never part of that equation.

The night before the second meeting with Sarah, I was seized by such a debilitating wave of terror that I faced just two options: to cancel the meeting or to ask Dan if he would come along. Pulling out, clearly, was impossible: I was the one who had sought Sarah out and now I had to grow up and deal with the consequences of that decision. Bringing Dan seemed far from ideal: surely the first people to meet Sarah from my inner circle ought to be Liam and Mary, or at the very least my siblings, Thérèse and David? But I knew instinctively that I could not introduce my family to Sarah at this stage. And so, the following morning, I called Catherine to let her know that I would be bringing Dan.

This time, instead of taking us upstairs to her office in Haddington Road, Catherine led us down the stairwell to a basement reception room sparsely furnished with four threadbare armchairs and a coffee table on which sat a box of Kleenex. The room was dreary and small with a low ceiling and exposed pipes. Dan, at six foot one, had to stoop slightly while entering. It felt like the sort of place in a hospital where you might sit with loved ones anticipating the worst.

We had arrived before Sarah. Catherine, cheery and friendly as always, left to make us cups of tea. I sat holding Dan's hand, crossing and uncrossing my legs, as nervous and queasy as I had been before the first meeting. I was glad of Dan's soothing presence, amazed at his agility and grace in stepping up to what amounted to significant new-girlfriend emotional baggage. 'My Irish saviour,' Dan would whisper frequently in those early weeks as he bent to kiss my head while I nestled in his arms. But the truth, as we sat waiting in that basement room, was that he was my saviour.

Catherine returned bearing a tray with four mugs of tea and a plate of biscuits – and, in her wake, Sarah. She looked different than before, softer, more polished; the fake-fur coat replaced by a smart jacket, her face clear of the bright blush that had given her a pantomime look. She smiled warmly when she saw me and held out her arms in delight. We were taken aback by her sudden appearance at the door and stood quickly, Dan pushing his armchair back with his knees and with great force knocking his head on the low pipe just above his head. The blow instinctively made him cry out in pain, and his hands moved quickly to the top of his forehead, where a nasty cut was already oozing blood. 'Oh Jesus, Dan, are ye all right?' said Catherine as she rushed to place the tray of tea on the coffee table. Sarah stood in shock, her hands across her mouth, horror etched across her face. I looked at her and then across at Dan, who was now smiling but embarrassed. I began to laugh. In that moment, with all of our collective attention focused on my sheepish and clumsy boyfriend, the ice was broken.

5

Sarah and I met a total of three times in the space of a few weeks in early 2000 at St Patrick's Guild. Over tea and biscuits the story of Sarah's life, and the unmarried pregnancy that threatened to ruin it, began to trickle out. It came to me in fragments, the picture building gradually and sometimes having to be revised, a testament to how fractured Sarah's mind was in the wake of the trauma she had suffered twenty-seven years before.

The raw outlines of the story of my own origins, as I grasped them in those first meetings at Haddington Road, were roughly as follows. In the late summer of 1971, in the provincial Irish town where she worked as a teacher, Sarah got pregnant by the man she was seeing. When Sarah sat him down in a local pub to tell him that she was pregnant, he didn't offer his support or deny that the child was his. He simply pretended not to hear her. Being unmarried, she felt she had to hide the pregnancy from her family, friends and colleagues. She gave up her job and fled to Dublin, where a Catholic agency gave her the address of a suburban house, the home of a young married couple. There, hidden away, Sarah helped care for the couple's young children while her belly swelled and swelled. I was born on a warm spring night in April 1972 and two days later dispatched to a 'baby home' in the city. Sarah went back to her job. Bereft, traumatized and burdened by the shame of her great, great sin, she never again spoke about the baby she surrendered to adoption.

When Sarah got the call from Catherine to say that I

wanted to make contact, she was weak with happiness. But there was a catch. In the intervening twenty-seven years, Sarah had told no one – not even the man she married or the children they raised – about the baby she'd carried and delivered in 1972. For Sarah, the secret was now so toxic, so enormous and all-encompassing, that revealing it threatened to destroy her world. She was terrified that her husband would leave her, that her children would shun her. At our second or third meeting, she asked that I cooperate in hiding my existence – temporarily – from her family and friends. I was eager to please and afraid of losing Sarah, so I agreed.

After the third meeting, mutually spooked by the dreary atmosphere at Haddington Road and by a sense that our conversations were somehow not entirely private, Sarah and I agreed that we should look for a new place to meet, and decided on the Westbury, a five-star hotel in the centre of Dublin. With high-backed armchairs and cloistered corners, the Westbury allowed a level of privacy and a hint of luxury that I found appealing. It was also familiar territory; in previous years, for a birthday treat or special outing, I had taken Mam to the same hotel for afternoon tea. Now, in what felt like an act of treachery, I began making assignations there with my other mother.

My second meeting with Sarah at the Westbury – which marked the beginning of what I came to think of as our affair – was also the last time I saw her before I took up a new job in The Hague. While working in Tuzla I had grown close to a team of investigators who travelled frequently to eastern Bosnia to collect evidence for the International Criminal Tribunal for the Former Yugoslavia. The investigators were an intense but friendly bunch from around the world, mostly police detectives and lawyers, and I enjoyed meeting them for dinner and drinks when they were in town. When it became clear that PHR was pulling out of Bosnia, a lead prosecutor offered me a job: to help draft a victim-impact statement and testimony on behalf of the Srebrenica community. The statement would form crucial evidence for the prosecution in the upcoming trial of a high-ranking Serbian general charged with genocide. I discussed my options with Dan and decided to take the job. We agreed for the time being to conduct a long-distance relationship. On 31 January 2000, I kissed Liam and Mary goodbye at Dublin airport and flew to Amsterdam, then boarded a train to The Hague.

Several weeks later, while cycling to the tribunal offices on a bike path in a wooded park, I found myself airborne, somersaulting over a car that had gone through a stop sign. Next I was crouched, cat-like, on my hands and knees. The pain was so intense that I knew I must be alive.

Around me I could hear screams and the slamming of car doors. A young man in a suit bent down low next to me. He spoke English with a strong South American accent. The path was still slick from rain the night before and I remember worrying that he would ruin his well-pressed trousers. I was breathing heavily now, trying to fight the unconsciousness that was closing in and the chilling realization that I could not feel my legs. In between gasps, I kept apologizing. For what, I'm not entirely sure. The man, in gentle whispers, kept telling me that everything was going to be OK. I thought back to Tuzla, where I had spent dark winter nights whizzing, helmetless, around the city streets on a shaky old racing bicycle. My Bosnian friends had tut-tutted at me for my recklessness but I had brushed off their concerns. Now, here I was, paralysed and dying among strangers in broad daylight in the safest cycling country in Europe.

I can still make Dan smile recounting the exact moment

when I realized that I would live: noticing, before I slipped into unconsciousness, the extraordinary good looks of one of the Dutch paramedics dispatched to help me.

In hospital I was told that the speed at which I had hit the car had caused my spine to compress in a dramatic manner. Although the feeling in my lower legs returned over the course of the next few days, I required major surgery – with bone harvesting and titanium plates – to reconstruct my spine, and to remove the shattered shards of vertebrae that were floating around my spinal canal. Lying immobile in a large body cast, I was unreachable in a fog of pain and morphine. On the fifth night following the accident, newly released from intensive care, I cried softly and told the night nurse in charge, a kindly woman from Ghana named Grace, that I wanted to die. I meant it: the pain at that point was unbearable. She held my hand, filled latex gloves with water to create balloons on which to cushion my excruciatingly painful feet and stayed next to me for hours. I will never forget her kindness.

Earlier on that fifth day, high as a kite on morphine, I had woken to see Pope John Paul II sitting next to my bed, knees crossed, hands in his lap. (Why my hallucinatory brain chose the then Pontiff and not Johnny Marr or Morrissey I still, to this day, do not understand.) The Pope smiled kindly at me as I came to, taking my hand in his and asking gently how I was feeling. His eyes were lively and kind, and I remember feeling benevolently serene and at peace. We chatted for some time – I can't remember what about – before he turned away slightly, still holding my hand, to look out of the window. We sat companionably like that before I fell asleep once again. Later that day, news of my papal visitor reached the head nurse. 'Decrease her morphine dosage,' the on-duty nurse was told.

The day following the accident, Dad and my brother, David, flew to The Hague to be with me. Mam, soon to be hospitalized in Dublin for surgery of her own, stayed behind. Dan, who had arrived in Holland for a visit three days before the accident, took the lead in conferring with the surgeons, signing insurance forms, relaying information to my family and calling my colleagues at the tribunal with progress reports. Hours following the accident, as I lay surrounded by medical technicians on a gurney in the ER, I had asked Dan to get in touch with my family, directing him first to call Thérèse so she could break the news in person to Mam and Dad. I wasn't sure whether to share the news with Sarah, knowing that she would be frantic with worry and that she had no one, apart from Catherine, to confide in. But keeping Sarah in the dark seemed cruel. It was clear that for the foreseeable future I would not be writing any letters and I would need to let Sarah know why. With no means of reaching her directly, I asked Dan to give Catherine a call.

A few weeks before the accident, I had returned home from work one evening to find a letter in my mail slot at the high-rise apartment building I was living in. It was from Sarah, forwarded by Catherine, a cheery handwritten response to my first note from the Netherlands updating her on my new life. I looked first to the top left-hand corner, where Sarah had written a return address, and felt my heart sink when I saw it was the address of St Patrick's Guild. Of course, I realized with disappointment, Sarah would not have given her real address: she didn't want a letter addressed to a mysterious 'Caitríona Palmer' being returned to her home, and she didn't want me writing to her there. From the start, we had been communicating via Haddington Road. But it was a disappointment to be reminded of this strange distance between us. At the same time, I luxuriated in the sight and slope of her handwriting, still finding everything about Sarah a novelty.

Dearest Caitríona,

How are you? Thank you so much for your lovely letter. 'Telepathy' again – we phoned Catherine on the same day. I was delighted to hear from you and to get all your news. It was really something else meeting you at Christmas and knowing that you are healthy, safe and happy. I'm so glad that you found me. My head was ready to burst at times wondering if you were OK. Now I know that you are more than OK and that everything is going your way. Dan is such a lovely fella. I'm delighted you found one another . . . I feel much happier now that you are in The Hague. I felt that bit uneasy about Bosnia . . . So until my next letter, lots and lots of love. Take your time in replying. No rush. Love to Dan.

Best wishes, Sarah xxxx

I still treasure this letter, keeping it in my diary next to the piece of A4 paper on which I first recorded the details of Sarah's life. It is one of the few letters that I have from Sarah in which she refers directly to my search for her and acknowledges her true feelings – in this case, her obvious relief in having been found. The tone is warm, friendly, responsive, just the way Sarah is in person. *I'm so glad that you found me. My head was ready to burst at times wondering if you were OK.* Those two sentences became my lifeline, irrefutable evidence that I had done the right thing.

Adoption reunion literature often refers to a 'honeymoon stage' following the initial meeting between a birth parent and child. Reunited parties often find themselves consumed by thoughts of the other, awash in love hormones. My immediate response to meeting Sarah was quite different, but something shifted quickly within me during our second meeting in the basement of Haddington Road, and by the time Dan and I left the building I was in full-blown honeymoon mode, blinded by a chemical rush of infatuation.

This ardour for Sarah persisted after I moved to The Hague and, once I had recovered from my accident sufficiently to travel home, I resumed wooing her with devotion and zeal. I couldn't get enough of her. She couldn't take her eyes off me. Being around her felt flirty and fun. It felt like falling in love.

At the same time, I felt Sarah's secrecy as a burden, and it quickly grew heavier. It may seem peculiar or creepy to compare my relationship with my birth mother to an extramarital affair, but it is the only analogy that works. In my mind, Sarah was the married lover, I her compliant mistress. I allowed Sarah, early on, to assume all the power: we met on her terms, during snatches of time when she could jettison her family responsibilities and sneak away. She never gave me her home address or telephone number. We relied on Catherine, our patient enabler, to pass messages back and forth and help broker the next secret assignation.

On my way to the Westbury, I would stop at a flower stand and buy bouquets of peonies, tulips and roses. Sarah's face would light up when she saw the flowers; she'd pause, bury her head inside the bouquet and inhale the scent. But it became clear that she had trouble explaining the flowers and other gifts back home, and so after a couple of months I stopped.

For her part, Sarah would give me cash, a couple of hundred euros crammed into a white envelope, my name scrawled on the front in blue pen. Once the tea and sandwiches had been served, she would reach into her handbag and produce the money.

'Here, buy yourself something nice,' she'd say, pushing the

envelope into my hands as I squirmed and protested. 'It's just a little something. Buy yourself a nice meal with a bottle of wine. It'll be lovely.'

The cash made me feel guilty, cheap and used, as though I was being paid off for my silence. But I spent it anyway – quickly and without much thought – on clothes and books, on an expensive pair of shoes, on the recommended 'nice meal' out. I often wondered if Sarah had to come up with an explanation for the money missing from her bank account. Did her husband pay attention to their finances?

Dublin is not a big city, and the risk of being discovered hung over every meeting. Early on, I broached the subject of what we should do if we ever ran into anyone we knew.

'Don't worry about it,' Sarah reassured me. 'We'll deal with that if it happens.'

Soon it did. One afternoon, as we were approaching one another in the lobby of the Westbury, Sarah breezed straight past me and into the embrace of a woman behind me. I stood frozen in shock. It took several seconds to compute what had just happened. In my pleasure to see Sarah I had not realized that her smile and gaze had been directed, not at me, but at the stranger over my shoulder; and that, in the presence of someone she knew, I had become suddenly invisible. I was devastated by the slight but also impressed by how artfully Sarah had carried it off. I wouldn't have thought she had it in her. My first instinct was to leave, but that would mean walking past Sarah and the mystery woman, now locked in animated conversation. Instead, my heart racing, I ducked behind a nearby pillar, waiting until the chatter sub-sided. A feeling of tightness began to spread across my chest, forcing me to take short, shallow breaths. My own mother had blanked me in broad daylight. I was six years old all over again, a bastard child lurking in shame.

When the woman walked away, I came out from behind the pillar.

'I'm so, so sorry about that,' Sarah said as we embraced and then climbed the stairs together towards the tea room. 'I didn't know what to do.'

'Not to worry,' I replied brightly, while trying to keep my devastation in check, 'it's totally fine.'

There was no mention of who the woman was, and I didn't dare ask. We stood in silence while the maître d' went to find a table. I couldn't remember ever feeling so small, so unlovable, so completely inconsequential.

Not long after that day, we jettisoned the tea and cakes and started meeting in the Westbury's bar, sipping late-afternoon gin and tonics in the darkest corner. I found these meetings emotionally punishing. Woozy from too much gin, I would return to Number 49 drained and spent, determined that we end the sneaking around once and for all. But the meetings were also addictive and, before long, with Catherine's help, we'd be arranging to meet again.

I wish now that I could have had the courage, in those early days, to take Sarah's delicate hands in mine, to look her in the eyes and say, gently, convincingly, with as much love as I could muster: 'This isn't working, Sarah. You can't treat me this way. I can't do this any more.' But as had been the case my entire life when faced with anything unpleasant or negative, I lacked the ability to say how I truly felt. Something in me made me avoid confrontation or uncomfortable truth-telling. I was always desperate to keep the peace. I reasoned, also, that it was I who had initiated the relationship, I who had intruded into Sarah's life, not the other way round; it wasn't for me to issue an ultimatum. And Sarah promised that she did not intend to keep my existence hidden for ever. And so I did not press Sarah in any depth about her reasons for keeping our relationship a secret, nor did I tell her just how destructive the secret was for me. I didn't tell her that, even in those enthralling, heart-fluttering first months, Sarah's secret was feeding a toxic thought that had dogged me my entire life: that I was simply not good enough, that I was undeserving of love, that I was worthless.

Navigating childhood as an adoptee was a little like living life as a refugee. In my new country I was grateful and often happy, but a persistent ache of otherness shadowed me from one day to the next.

Some experts separate adopted children into two categories: the attention-seeking child who acts out and gives her adoptive parents hell, and the compliant, easy-going adoptee who constantly seeks approval. Growing up, I fell firmly into the latter category. At an early age, determined to do Liam and Mary proud, I made the decision that I would become the best little girl that I could possibly be. I was polite, pleasant and eager to please. Aware that I was 'special', I applied myself diligently to meeting expectations. Adept at gauging emotions, I learned quickly how to scan a room, assessing which adult or child needed the most attention. I made eye contact, shook hands and drew murmurs of approval and delight from all the grown-ups I met. I was the child that other parents wanted their offspring around, the good girl, the kid who could teach others a thing or two about manners. I never let the side down.

I ran with a large group of friends, played hide and seek and 'kick stone' in the road, and spun endless cartwheels on the grassy slopes of my friend Áine Mulchay's back garden. I played peacemaker when friends fell out. The fact that I was adopted rarely came up amongst my peers. Once I remember silencing an escalating shouting match between two friends trying to one up the other. *Oh yeah, well I'm adopted!* I remember saying as their astonished heads swivelled towards mine. The attention felt surprisingly good.

I became obsessed with orphaned figures – Paddington Bear, Annie, Oliver Twist. Their stories moved me deeply, spoke to me on a cellular level. Paddington – with his ratty suitcase and torn luggage tag imploring someone, anyone, to *Please look after this bear* – became a role model of sorts. He was polite and solicitous, just like me. He was desperate to please, just like me. He had found salvation and a home with a new family but nevertheless, cognizant of his outsider status, he tiptoed through life, forever fearful of losing the good fortune that he had found.

My sense of dislocation haunted me most vividly at night. I remember a period in the late 1970s when I cried myself to sleep, catatonic with grief, asking over and over again for a nameless, unseen mother. I lay under my Paddington duvet cover and let the tears fall while whispering the song 'Where is Love?' from the hit movie musical *Oliver!* The lyrics spoke to me: 'Where is she? Who I close my eyes to see? Will I ever know the sweet hello that's meant for only me?' Even then, I knew that I was being dramatic, but I couldn't help it. The grief and the sorrow felt real and the weeping was a release. It felt as though my mystery mother was imprinted in my psyche, embedded in my DNA. But I knew to stifle my sobs as soon as I heard footsteps on the carpeted stairwell. It would be the ultimate betrayal for Mam to hear my pitiful pleas for the sought-after comforting arms of my other mother.

Sometimes I was so fixated on playing the good girl, on satisfying the needs of others, that I skirted close to danger. Aged eleven, I complied when a plump and sweaty priest made a show of handpicking me to sit next to him on a pilgrimage bus in southern France and, with a brazenness that still astounds me, kept his roving and chubby fingers up the trousers of my wide-legged shorts for most of the two-hour bus ride. I acquiesced around the same time when an elderly parishioner in Raheny hugged me too close while Liam and Mary were in the adjacent kitchen making tea, holding me tightly by the shoulders while we stood and watched the evening news, his bony fingers flickering over the buds of my emerging breasts while his lower body methodically ground against mine. I smiled and said yes when a lone jogger approached my friend Ruth and me one afternoon while we played on the sand dunes at Dollymount Strand, asking if we would hold down his legs while he did sit-ups to tighten his flabby belly. We knelt in the sand, our heads opposite the other, and obediently did as we were told, wide-eyed and repulsed by the sight of the engorged purple penis that protruded through a hole in his tiny running shorts. Plenty of my non-adopted friends have recounted similar tales of wandering priestly fingers and inappropriate touching while sitting on the laps of older men, but I believe that predators detected my peculiar eagerness to please.

Unsure of my place in life, and desperate to prove my self-worth, I became an over-achiever. Armed with good exam results and a glowing reference from the nuns at my convent school, I was the first member of the household to go to university. In 1993, Liam and Mary, dressed to the nines, beamed as I was awarded my honours degree in history and politics from University College Dublin. A year and a half later I won a prestigious Fulbright scholarship to study for my master's at Boston College.

I was, I suppose, officially a success. I had also, by the time I left for the United States, passed a test: making it to adult-hood without the calamity of an unplanned pregnancy.

79

Although Mary never said so explicitly, I intuitively under-stood her fear that my murky DNA marked me apart from my peers, that I was predisposed to repeat the catastrophic mistake of my biological parents. By avoiding that fate, I had done Liam and Mary proud, a fact often mentioned by fam-ily friends and relatives in a tone that suggested they'd believed that the Palmer adoption fairy tale might not turn out so well.

But beneath my polished, polite veneer, I hummed with emptiness, with the feeling that I was somehow incomplete. I was constantly on edge, terrified that if I allowed my people-pleasing mask to drop, somebody might discover the fraud lurking beneath. I felt lost in my own skin, neither Liam and Mary's child nor that of the woman who had given me away. Intellectually, even as a child, I understood why an unmarried Irish mother in 1972 might feel compelled to give her child away. But no amount of rationalization helped. The facts were clear: my own mother had abandoned me. Per-haps I had not been good enough to keep?

In my late teens and early twenties, I made calamitous romantic choices, pursuing elusive, emotionally unavailable men. I equated commitment with self-worth and mistook passion for love, craving the intensity of touch, of eye con-tact, of physical connection. Terrified of rejection, I placed my own needs last. I was a doormat, someone to be walked over. When these men left, as inevitably they did, the rejec-tion was paralysing. Humiliated, I pursued them again with vigour, doing anything to woo them back. The cycle was exhausting and self-destructive.

In her memoir *The Mistress's Daughter*, A. M. Homes writes about her feelings of dislocation as an adoptee: 'To be adopted is to be adapted, to be amputated and sewn back together again. Whether or not you regain full function, there will always be scar tissue.' My friend Claire, an Irish adoptee and fellow St Patrick's Guild alumna, compared her adoption to a grafting procedure, whereby she was the shoot taken from a parent tree and grafted on to another. Even when the graft is a success, Claire told me, it is never seamless.

My graft to Liam and Mary did take, but I was rife with scar tissue. Over the years I compiled a store of suppressed rage. By the time I reached my mid twenties, if I drank too much my brain would sometimes flood with a tingly and disorientating warmth and I would suddenly find my voice and use it, with devastating effect, typically on those I loved. At the same time, I had no insight into the source of my feelings.

Once, in early 1998, following an earth-shattering row with Chris, as we sat shell-shocked on the front steps of our apartment in Boston, he suggested that I talk to someone about the anger. 'I think you need to look into it, to find out where it is coming from,' he said gently, taking my hand in his. 'Perhaps,' he suggested, 'it's something to do with being adopted.'

Even then, astonished and ashamed by the maelstrom I had just unleashed, I shook my head and demurred.

'It's not my adoption,' I told him, fully believing what I was about to say. 'I think I'm just unhappy at work.'

6

For the first several years of our relationship, Sarah was evasive when I probed for information about her past life, painting nothing but the broadest strokes in a landscape that seemed barren and devoid of colour. Too shy to push aggressively for details, I survived on only the skimpiest of facts: that Sarah grew up on Ireland's western seaboard, a place that was both breathtakingly beautiful but also viciously windswept and isolated; that her parents were cottage farmers, working long hours on their smallholding; and that life was hard but happy. I understood too from the pained and hesitant way that Sarah spoke about her parents that she did not like to revisit her childhood and that, for whatever reason, it required great mental energy for her to conjure up the past.

In the early years I tried to suppress my appetite for information, hoping to win Sarah over with my patience. Every now and then she would throw me a bone, telling an amusing story about her siblings: the time her brother nearly fell off a cliff into the sea or the winter when most of the kids refused to eat their beloved – and freshly slaughtered – family pig. 'Nobody would eat the meat because the pig had turned into a pet,' Sarah told me, smiling. 'This fellow came along to kill it and you could hear the squeals, so nobody wanted it. There was just one brother who ate the lot. He would pile it on to the plate. Pile it on.' Later, heading back to Number 49 on the train, I would unpack these stories in my mind and wallow in their imagery, building a composite picture of the ancestral homestead that I had not yet visited, but where I yearned to go one day with Sarah.

She told me that the woman who would become her mother, Mairéad, was working as a housemaid in the north of England when she came home to attend her sister's wedding. The man who would become Sarah's father, Seán, had just inherited the family farm. During the wedding feast, furtive glances were exchanged; the following day a message was sent to the local matchmaker. Mairéad returned briefly to England to pack up her life and took the boat train back to Ireland. The marriage lacked any great romance or sentimentality, but Sarah remembers her parents coexisting agreeably in their tiny farmhouse, her mother tending to the children and small animals, her father working on the land, taking care of the livestock and spending afternoons in a long, narrow boat fishing for mackerel, pollock and lobsters. The mackerel caught in summer were gutted, cleaned, smothered in salt and placed in a huge barrel that would feed the family through the winter months. Sarah remembers eating the briny fish for breakfast on school mornings, along with a glass of warm milk from the family cow. This fuelled her for the mile-and-a-half-long walk along the hedgerowed lanes towards the local two-roomed national school.

The stone house where the family lived was modest, but comfortable, with two floors and three small bedrooms. A chilly outhouse across the courtyard was shared by Sarah's family and the family next door. Downstairs was a small living space with a basic kitchen and a large range on which my grandmother made functional meals: boiled pig's head and feet, cabbage and potatoes, soda bread and apple tart. A field close to the house yielded all the vegetables – potatoes, onions, cabbages – that the family required.

All week long Sarah looked forward to Friday afternoons

and the moment when, newly released from school, she would run to the local shop to buy the weekly edition of her favourite comics, *Judy* and *Bunty*. Friday nights, before bed, Sarah and her siblings received their most anticipated weekly treat: thick slabs of shop bread smothered in butter and jam. On special occasions they got a cake or a bottle of squash. 'You'd tear one another apart,' Sarah recalled, remembering the tussle between the siblings over the coveted treats. Twice a week, a local bus took Sarah's mother and other local women across the heath, past the sheep grazing on rocky hills, into a larger town and a more expansive cluster of shops.

Gentle and soft-spoken and with no stomach for some of the harsher realities of farm life, Mairéad would occasionally ask Sarah or her siblings to run and fetch a neighbour to twist the neck of a chicken. A couple of hundred yards away from the house stood a well with a mechanical pump. Sarah remembers her mother trudging back and forth, her head stooped under the weight of the overflowing buckets which sloshed noisily in both hands. Back in the kitchen, Mairéad would stoke the fire and boil a large pot of water to scrub the family's clothes. Sometimes, on her return from school, Sarah would find a sick calf resting beside the fire in the kitchen or a box of young chicks perched perilously close to the family cat. 'You'd have to keep an eye on the chicks because other-wise they'd just disappear,' she told me once, laughing with the memory. 'I'm sure they were very tasty. I can still see them, a whole load of them in the box by the fire.'

There were two strands to the family's spiritual life. On Sunday mornings, decked out in her freshly starched 'good clothes', Sarah would walk with her family to Mass in the church two miles away. She dreaded Mass; but she was very interested in the fairies who lurked in the fields and the hedgerows. The fairies played tricks on people, stealing food from the pantry and pots and pans from the hearth. They kidnapped young women from their homes, causing mothers to go wild with worry while the menfolk combed the land searching in vain for their missing daughters. The girls would invariably turn up again but they were never the same – evasive, lost in thought, damaged for ever by the ethereal goings-on in the fairy kingdom. Sometimes, Sarah told me, the fairies were said to foretell death, illuminating the ditches around the house of the dying with a strange light that would disappear as soon as the ailing inhabitant inside took their last breath. Her parents had heard stories, generations old, of other villagers who had watched behind closed curtains as the fairies held silent funerals in the dead of night, holding their breath with terror until the sombre procession filed past. Other times, the fairies were said to be the cause of death, exacting retribution for amorphous crimes or snubs against their fairy lords, like the young father from a neighbouring village who was dispatched while fishing one afternoon to a watery grave, in vengeance, it was said, for deliberately knocking down the circular mound – or fairy fort – that stood in the middle of his land. Scrambling over the stone walls and scrubby fields that ringed her childhood home, Sarah learned early on to avoid the fairy forts. She did not believe the abduction stories that the grown-ups whispered to one another around the hearth at night, but even so, it made sense not to tempt fate. 'You'd keep away from it,' she told me. 'You had these superstitions.' Even the mere hint of scepticism could be enough to invite the wrath of the fairy kingdom and so Sarah, like the good girl she was raised to be, kept her doubts to herself.

Sarah spent the summer months roaming the fields and playing on the sandy beach that lay at the end of a sloping lane near her home. The braver and more boisterous of the village kids spent sunny afternoons launching themselves off the side of the pier and into the chilly water below, drawing shouts from the local fishermen to mind the nets and lobster pots. There was barely any adult supervision but no one seemed to care. 'You came home when you were hungry,' Sarah remembers.

In many ways, the picture Sarah painted of her childhood reflected the romanticized post-war vision of Ireland that Taoiseach Éamon de Valera drew in his famous 1943 St Patrick's Day speech, when he spoke of his desire for a land 'bright with cosy homesteads', 'the romping of sturdy children', and 'the laughter of happy maidens'. But the reality was that by the mid 1950s, when Sarah was starting school, Ireland was in the economic doldrums, ridden with unemployment and mass emigration. As the firstborn male in his family, Sarah's father inherited the ancestral farm upon the death of his father. But many of his siblings, unable to make a living, packed up and left for the port of Cobh with a one-way steerage ticket for New York. Some, like a younger brother who died soon after making it to Massachusetts, never returned. The others fanned out across the United States, earning decent lives as builders, nurses and teachers. Sarah told me about the excitement at home when the postman, twice yearly, would deliver a fat brown envelope from America, stuffed with dollars. She told me too of the jittery anticipation of the lead-up to Christmas, when bulky parcels would begin to arrive at the steps of the stone house, postmarked Boston and New York, and full of dresses, shirts and shoes. 'There was a beautiful smell from the clothes,' she said. 'You could smell it for weeks afterwards.' If the shoes were too big, Sarah's mother would stuff the toes with cotton wool. On Christmas Eve, the children would be sent to the beach to fill a jam jar with sand. At home, Sarah's parents would place a red candle in the middle of the jar and light it before Midnight Mass. The following day, Santa Claus would deliver small gifts; little dolls for Sarah and her sisters, toy guns with caps for the boys. Christmas dinner would be a plump turkey, a gift from Sarah's aunt.

Although Sarah grew up alongside girls whose destiny was marriage, not university, her mother was, in Sarah's words, 'really into education', instilling in each of her daughters the idea that knowledge was a potential passport to a better life. A precocious and gifted student, Sarah quickly won praise and attention from her primary school teachers. When she was twelve years old, they encouraged her to apply for a scholarship to a convent boarding school a few counties away. Sarah passed the entrance exam with flying colours and the following September she took the bus across the hills towards her new life. Although the corridors of the convent were cold and dimly lit, Sarah loved the place, luxuriating in the roomy expanse of her new dormitory, relieved to be no longer sharing cramped quarters with her many siblings back home. In the mornings, she attended Mass with her class-mates in the convent chapel, ate breakfast in a large refectory beneath an enormous crucifix, then scurried to classes and the study hall. Every Sunday, she and her classmates took a stroll through the local village, walking in a long single line with a nun at each end. At Christmas, Easter and the start of each summer, a minibus pulled up at the gates of the school to take her home.

In 2010, during lunch at a hotel in Dublin, Sarah reached over to rummage into her large handbag. I expected her to pull out the usual white envelope stuffed with cash. Instead, she placed several sheets of A4 paper in my hands.

'Here you go,' she said with a smile. 'Have a look at these.'

I looked down. The first page was headed 'Eulogy'. I quickly scanned the first paragraph, which described a man whose surname was Sarah's maiden name.

'That was my father's brother,' Sarah said. 'He died last year and his daughter wrote this eulogy. She makes lots of references to his childhood. I thought you'd find it interesting.'

Sarah then pointed to the other papers in my hands. 'The rest,' she said, 'are a couple of photos from home.'

My heart skipped a beat. Sarah had waited nearly five years before showing me a photograph of two of her three children, my half-siblings, omitting, for reasons I never understood, a photograph of her daughter. Another time she handed me a small memorial card for a long-deceased uncle, a picture of John Paul II on the front and the Sacred Heart on the back with a grainy photograph of the uncle. I took the memorial card home, unsure of what to do with it, feeling no connection whatsoever to the man it memorialized. It felt to me as though Sarah was trying to keep my curiosity about closer family members at bay by feeding me a bare minimum of information.

But this time felt different and I stared with disbelief at the goldmine sitting in my hands. Sarah leant over and pulled out a piece of paper from the pile. In the middle of the page was a photograph – neatly photocopied – of a young man holding a baby, the child voluminously swaddled in white christening robes, practically invisible save for a glimpse of a tiny snub nose – my nose – and a shock of jet-black hair.

'That's me,' Sarah said, 'with my father. I'm just a few weeks old.'

I looked down at the photograph, my heart racing. Staring back at me, a lopsided grin on his tanned, welcoming face, was Sarah's father, my biological grandfather. It was the first time I had ever laid eyes on him. I felt my body flood with a rush of adrenaline, a sensation that I feel every time I see a photograph of a hitherto unknown biological relative. Wearing a black cap, the peak pulled jauntily to the left, Seán looked confident, happy. He was broad-shouldered and handsome, despite a prominent nose and overbite. In his arms he held a newborn Sarah rather awkwardly, out towards the camera, her head resting against the left side of his chest, his left arm supporting her weight. Behind him, the old stone house was bathed in bright afternoon sunlight, the first hint of a triangular shadow creeping along the lower half. Looking at this image, I had two immediate feelings: an instant affinity towards this smiling paternal stranger and a sense that Sarah, as a baby, looked eerily similar to me.

The next page in the pile was a group photograph. Judging by the clothes they were wearing – the women in high-collared buttoned cotton dresses, the men in peaked caps and woollen suits – it looked to be the late 1800s. Their heads were all turned quizzically to the right, as though a sudden commotion across the fields had caught their attention. Nobody looked happy. An enormous haycock bulged obscenely in the background. To the left was a neatly stacked pile of cut turf, to the right a low stone wall. In the middle of the group sat a woman who commanded my immediate attention. She was straight-backed, stern, her long hair pulled into a tight bun, her giant hands resting on her lap. She looked like someone you would be well advised not to mess with. 'That's your great-great-grandmother,' said Sarah.

Next, two separate photographs showed a pair of cherubic blonde toddlers, a boy and a girl. They looked like twins. 'That's me,' Sarah said, pointing to the little girl. 'That's my cousin,' her finger resting lightly on the head of the little boy. Sarah, as a toddler, was adorable – edible. She had long blonde curls, chubby cheeks and pudgy sausage fingers. In one photograph she wore a white three-quarter-length dress that was a little grubby around the hems. She was holding the hand of her barefoot cousin, his tiny chest puffed out with importance and his eyes trained defiantly on the camera. Sarah was looking shyly at the ground, her tiny hand clutching a swatch of her dress, her beautiful smile – a feature I love so much in her adult self – lifting her cheeks into delicious rounds of perfection.

I realized as I sat with Sarah, our heads bent together over a bunch of grainy old photographs, that I had never felt happier in her company. The moment felt natural, pure, unhurried. For once, we were simply mother and daughter, poring over pictures of relatives long dead. Fretful that the easeful mood would soon dissipate, I posed more questions, desperate not just for more information but for the comfort of her undivided attention. For once, Sarah had unlocked the door to her life, to my past, and let me in.

Mam was the first to acknowledge the irony that my biological relatives were poor, rural, mostly Irish-speaking farmers. 'It's clear you didn't lick that up from the stones,' she said one day when I mentioned Sarah's fluency in the Irish language, a justified dig at my own appalling grasp of the national mother tongue. Sarah was only a short generation older than me, but it wasn't until that moment in 2010, when I was confronted with photographic evidence of her past, that I properly grasped how different the world that formed her was from the world I grew up in.

Although Liam had an intimate knowledge of the roads and lanes criss-crossing Ireland, our family rarely left the city, and certainly never for holiday breaks. I can remember only two times in my childhood when we daringly travelled into the 'country': once to meet friends of Liam's, musicians from a colliery band in northern England, for a weekend jaunt on the River Shannon, and another time when we went to see the same English family in Donegal. Although there were farmers in the family – Mam's clan, land owners from Tipperary, had migrated to Dublin in the late 1800s – as children my siblings and I gravitated more towards the stories handed down from Dad's side. His father, Alfred Palmer, had moved from England to Dublin as a young child in the early 1900s. He fought in the First World War and returned to Dublin in 1918 suffering from shell shock, a young man turned prematurely old and with feet rotted by trench mud. I remember bringing photographs of Alfred in uniform into school, standing proudly on the podium next to my teacher as I recounted how his cavalry horse at Ypres had been pulverized beneath him by a German artillery shell. I spoke about his bouts of dysentery and typhoid, and how he had maintained some semblance of respectability in the trenches by shaving each winter day with a tin cup brimming with muddy snow water. I knew too about his conversion to the Catholic faith and how one Sunday afternoon in 1920 he begged the Virgin Mary during benediction at Clarendon Street church in Dublin's city centre to cure his rotting feet, promising that if she did he would attend Sunday benediction every day for the rest of his life, a pledge he honourably carried out until just before his death in 1974. Alfred's outsider status spoke to me and I decided early on that I would be a Palmer shaped in the mould of this quiet, unassuming, hardworking man. As a teenager I mined family members' memories for details on his life, absorbing every fact, internalizing every story.

My beloved aunt Carmel, Liam's only sister, once told me that Alfred and my grandmother, Mary, kept a tea tray commemorating the 1953 coronation of Queen Elizabeth hidden from view in their tiny two-up two-down terraced house on Ferns Road in Crumlin. Discerning visitors to Ferns Road – those who were not at all fazed by the Palmers' attachment to the British royal family – would be served tea and cakes against a reproduction of Elizabeth II and the yellow, red and blue backdrop of the royal standard. Carmel's story reminded me of the stainless-steel tray with the iconic engagement photograph of Prince Charles and Lady Diana Spencer – her bejewelled left arm placed defensively across her blue-suited waist, his hand proprietorially on her shoulder – that somehow turned up at Number 49 in 1981 and that was kept out of view. I learned early on, as a child growing up in 1980s Dublin while the Troubles raged in the North, that there were some people to whom I should not serve tea on this particular tray.

The radio in the kitchen at Number 49 was always tuned to RTÉ 1, but in the 'good room', the living and dining room that my parents spent a small fortune extending and refurbishing in the early 1980s, Liam would listen to BBC radio. This room, kept like a shrine, was officially off limits for us kids except when we had special visitors. But Liam often let me join him there, the stereo playing Bach, Handel, Britten, Elgar and the British military and colliery band music that he loves so much. On summer nights, we listened to the BBC for the Proms music series from the Royal Albert Hall, culminating in the last night when, sitting on Liam's lap, I would bounce along to Elgar's March No. 1, *Pomp and Circumstance*.

There was no conflict in our household between Anglophilia and devout Catholicism. When I was ten years old, Dad took me to Coventry, where we slept overnight on the airport runway, with 300,000 other pilgrims, to await the arrival the following morning of Pope John Paul II. Later that week, in London, we sat in the highest row of the Albert

Hall to listen to the London Symphony's performance of Tchaikovsky's *1812 Overture*. I remember gripping Dad's arm in sudden terror towards the end, startled by the booming cannon fire.

Every evening after school, just before the bells of the Angelus rang out on RTÉ, I was dispatched around the corner to the local newsagent, fifty pence in hand, to buy a copy of the *Evening Herald*. On weekends, in addition to the Irish Sunday newspapers, Dad would buy – on special order – the British papers, delivered to Ireland by airmail from London. Every month the postman delivered the *British Bandsman*, reviewing the latest news and performances of the colliery and military bands across the UK. Dad regretted that he had never had the chance to play trumpet in an Irish army band, but he spent vast sums of money to send his children every Saturday morning to the College of Music on Chatham Row, where Thérèse, David and I received rigorous instruction in musical theory and an instrument of our choice. At home, most afternoons, Mam would have to browbeat me into practising my cornet, sending me to the chilly bathroom upstairs. I would open the hot press, prop my sheet music against the neatly folded towels and sheets, and aim my instrument into the gloom of the cupboard – the idea being that the linens would muffle the noise and keep the neighbours from complaining.

Because of Liam's job, our family was entitled to free rail and ferry travel, and so every summer we boarded a Sealink ferry in Dún Laoghaire harbour that took us across the Irish Sea to Holyhead. Liam and Mary would settle into the premier lounge on the upper deck while my siblings and I were allowed to roam the ship, the MV *St Columba*, at will. I remember the joy and freedom of that three-hour crossing, running up and down the centre stairs of the ferry, darting through the high-backed chairs in the bar and dangling, head first, over the side rails of the top deck, my short hair blowing in the salty breeze. At Holyhead we boarded a train for London, sitting in a reserved carriage where we extracted ham and salad sandwiches from tinfoil and drank sugary tea out of enormous flasks. About an hour before arriving into Euston station, my stomach would begin to flutter with stirrings of anxiety. Every year the scene was the same: two adults, three children, five suitcases and a multitude of smaller bags containing buckets and spades and packets of biscuits, crisps, bottles of lemonade, flasks of tea. Our cumbersome circus never failed to irritate London commuters as we made our bumbling way down the tube escalators – keeping to the right, of course.

The Northern Line brought us to Waterloo, where we boarded another train to Bournemouth. By nightfall we were in our B & B, a narrow, dimly lit Victorian house that was a twenty-minute walk from the beach. Unable to pronounce the name of the Polish man, Mr Kruszynski, who ran the place with his English wife, we referred to our hosts fondly as 'Mr and Mrs K', greeting them every morning in the dining room at the back of the house where they would serve tiny glasses of chilled grapefruit or orange juice, plates of sausages, bacon and eggs, and little stainless-steel trays of triangular toast. We spent the rest of the day on the beach, playing in the sand and jumping in and out of the chilly surf. I was indulged with pony rides, games of 'crazy golf', trampoline sessions and as much ice cream as I could possibly consume. In the afternoons we would walk to the bandstand in the Lower Gardens or wander through the busy high street. Back at the B & B we would be served dinner by Mr K, starting the meal with the same tiny glass of orange or grapefruit juice that we had been served at breakfast. I raced through it all to get to dessert, vanilla ice cream with strawberry jelly or little pots layered with fruit, custard and cream with a maraschino cherry, the greatest of all treats, sitting on top.

Once, Mr K, dressed in an apron, his white shirtsleeves rolled partway up his arms, stretched across our dinner table to set down a plate of food. As he reached, the sleeve on his left arm rode up, revealing, in my direct line of sight, a dark vertical line of numbers tattooed down the slope of his inner forearm.

'What are those numbers on his arm?' I remember asking Mam and Dad as I watched Mr K return to the kitchen to collect more dishes from his wife. The question hung out there as my parents exchanged glances across the table. 'Eat your dinner,' came the response.

7

'I used to think of your birth mother as bad, wondering why would someone want to do that? That it was terrible to abandon a child,' said my sister, Thérèse. 'I must have been a teenager before I kind of copped on, before I realized that she wasn't bad, that she had just made a terrible mistake.'

I am sitting round the dining-room table of Thérèse's house in Malahide, a picturesque suburb by the sea in north County Dublin. It is February 2011 and outside it is ferociously cold, the wind whipping across the estuary of the River Broadmeadow. Every now and then a gust of wind rattles the double-insulated doors on Thérèse's tidy front porch, but in the dining room the temperature is borderline tropical. On the table are the remains of our Sunday 'tea' – roast beef sandwiches, leftovers from the tenderloin we feasted on earlier for lunch, a pavlova and an apple tart fresh from Mam's oven at Number 49. In the kitchen, framed by the window overlooking Thérèse's neat back garden, stands my brother-in-law Paul, his head bent over the sink washing dishes; to my right sits Thérèse; and across from us, a cup of tea in one hand, is Mam. Dad is at the head of the table, recently returned from the living room where the televised football highlights – his mandatory weekend viewing – have just ended. This is my entire immediate family, save for my brother, David, who lives in England.

For the past couple of years I have been nurturing the idea of writing a book about my search for Sarah, about her life and her secret, and about my intense and strange relationship with her. On a sudden impulse I have travelled home alone to Dublin for a week, leaving my husband and children behind in Washington. But now that I am here, I am not exactly sure what type of research I should be undertaking. The idea of writing a book seems half-baked – I have no outline, no publisher. But I know that I need to get my story – and Sarah's – down on paper. And in order to do that, I must first talk to Mam and Dad.

On the table before us, between a plate of chocolate biscuits and a pot of tea, sits my black Sony digital tape recorder, one of the tools of my trade as a journalist. Mam eyes it warily, and its appearance alters the atmosphere in the room. Dad sits up straighter in his chair while Thérèse gets up to close the door between the dining room and kitchen, where Paul can still be heard clanking dishes. I feel unusually nervous, the same feeling I've had when sitting down with senior government officials or the Irish President for one-on-one interviews. I could just talk to my family about this topic like a normal person, but I feel the need to position myself as journalist, to place as much emotional distance as possible between me and the past. It feels a bit ridiculous that even now, at thirty-nine years of age, I lack the courage to look my parents in the eye and talk in a natural way about my adoption. They have been nothing but generous with information in the past, despite their generational aversion to tricky emotional subjects. The reticence and shyness is mine, causing me to masquerade as a journalist in my sister's home, to hide behind a machine.

'So,' I begin, 'I thought it would be interesting to interview you all. To talk about the adoption process, you know, how you got me, how it all began.' I lean across the table to hit the 'start' button and watch as the red record light comes on.

'I'm not sure where we should start. Perhaps the moment when you decided that you should adopt?'

Mary was sad and adrift when, in September 1971, she returned to Number 49 following the ectopic rupture that caused the loss of her pregnancy and required a period of recuperation in hospital. Liam had done a good job of keeping the house afloat while Mary was away, helped by a coterie of neighbours and his sister-in-law, Pat, who had married Liam's twin, James, a couple of years earlier and now lived five minutes down the road with their young son. As the winter of 1971 approached, Mary tried to get back into the swing of things: taking the kids to school, stopping off on the way home for Mass at Raheny church and a quick run around the aisles at the local supermarket, H. Williams. Back at home she would climb over the low stone wall dividing Number 49 and Number 51 to have a cup of tea, a biscuit or two and a chat with our next-door neighbour Bríd. (In the afternoon, Bríd would make the return journey across the same wall for a reciprocal cuppa and plate of biscuits.) Saturdays were spent running errands and taking Thérèse and David to music practice. Sundays were reserved for Mary's widowed father, who would alight from a double-decker bus round the corner on Howth Road at 12.45 p.m. sharp, dapper in a dark suit, silk tie and Italian leather shoes, expecting to be served his weekly platter of roast meat, potatoes, peas and gravy fifteen minutes later.

Mary was off-kilter that winter, undermined by the damage that the ectopic rupture had wrought on her reproductive organs, exhausted and drained by a persistent flow of vaginal bleeding. In late October, nearly a month following the miscarriage, Mary was once again back in hospital, weakened by blood loss, and was told she would need a hysterectomy. She was devastated, hoping against hope that there was some alternative, but the doctors were adamant. 'Look,' one insistent doctor told Liam following another operation to stop the haemorrhaging, 'we're going to have to remove that womb.'

If there was going to be another child in the family, adoption now appeared to be the only option. But Mary worried that an adoption agency would be reluctant to give a newborn child to a prospective parent who was about to undergo major abdominal surgery. She told Liam she would put the hysterectomy on the long finger. She wanted to adopt, to give a precious little baby a chance at a wonderful life and in turn help out the poor child's mother. It felt like the right thing to do. Mary knew what they would call an adopted baby girl: Caitríona, in honour of Saint Catherine Labouré, the patron saint of the miraculous medal who, as a little girl, had lost her own mother.

A couple across the street had adopted two gorgeous little boys – one dark-haired, the other ginger – and the woman had never seemed happier. And Mary and Liam's friend Seán Gaynor and his wife had adopted through a Catholic agency on Middle Abbey Street – St Patrick's something-or-other. Mary decided that she would start there.

On 29 April 1922, a package was dispatched from Number 50, Middle Abbey Street, in the centre of Dublin, to the neo-Gothic building in Drumcondra where the Most Reverend Edward Byrne DD, the Archbishop of Dublin, presided. The package contained the 1920 annual report for St Patrick's Guild – a charity established ten years earlier to help 'indigent' and 'unwanted' children – and a letter, written by one Miss M. J. Cruice, the honorary secretary and founder of the Guild, begging His Grace's forgiveness for her tardiness in submitting the report. 'I delayed out of consideration not wishing to trespass on you at a time when you were concerned with matters of greater importance,' she wrote in reference, perhaps, to the turbulent months following the signature of the Anglo-Irish Treaty in December 1921, which ended the War of Independence and allowed for the establishment of a self-governing Irish free state.

Founded with the motto 'Save the Child', St Patrick's Guild pledged to rescue both women and children, including orphans, the 'crippled or mentally deficient', and the 'destitute'. Although the Guild claimed to offer assistance to all of these unhappy creatures (with the exception of the 'habitually sinful'), it was the unmarried mother who occupied a special place in Miss Cruice's heart. These women, Miss Cruice wrote to Archbishop Byrne in 1927, were 'of every class, from the professional man's daughter to the peasant's. Some were highly educated, others were grossly ignorant and in most cases very ignorant of their religion. About 15% were mentally deficient and quite 50% a little abnormal.' Maintaining the sexual double standard that Sarah would encounter decades later, there was no mention of the putative father: all of the moral culpability that accompanied a pregnancy out of wedlock seemed to rest upon the woman.

In her 1922 report, under the heading 'Method of the Guild in Dealing with these Cases', Miss Cruice explained the various methods of keeping unmarried pregnant women hidden from sight:

When . . . such cases are recommended to the Guild by a Priest, Nun, Catholic Doctor, Vincent de Paul Brother, etc. the girl is dealt with in such a way as to save her good name, give her a new start in life under religious influence and assure the future of her child.

While awaiting her confinement she is placed as a respectable girl in some lodging or if possible she is secured a position involving only light work. For her confinement she is sent to a Maternity Hospital – then mother and child are separated as soon as it is practicable and before the mother-love becomes too strong. The mother then, her fame intact, is sent home to her parents if this be possible or else she is secured some position suitable to her training and capacities. She is required – and is generally found most willing – to set apart some of her earnings for her child's support. Meanwhile the child is put to Nurse with some respectable family . . . In choosing them, regard is always had, of course, for the religious character of the foster mother.

After a period of generally about three years, sometimes very much longer, a more permanent provision is made for the child. Very often its adoption is arranged for by means of money received from its mother, father, or other relatives, or when such resources fail, by means of the Guild's funds. Often the foster-parents, having grown fond of the child, offer to adopt it gratuitously. Where adoption is not possible the child is placed in an Industrial School or Orphanage.

The unmarried mothers who approached St Patrick's Guild might have been 'of every class', but Miss Cruice had a preference for women who could pay their way. In the Guild's annual report of 1939, which includes a table summarizing that year's applicants seeking assistance, the majority came from the middle or landed class. Those in the table listed as 'domestic servant' or 'factory worker' were invariably turned away and referred elsewhere, usually to St Patrick's Home, Pelletstown, a public institution for unmarried mothers. In 1935, Father Condon of the Pro-Cathedral in Marlborough

Street complained in a letter to the Archbishop's secretary that Miss Cruice was charging 10/– a week to board out children when foster mothers were receiving only 7/6 a week for the same work. 'I had a few stand-up fights with Miss Cruice during my term of office,' Father Condon wrote, 'for trying to push on cases to me where no money was available. "Nothing for nothing" should be the motto of St Patrick's Guild.'

The fear of 'proselytization' – that Catholic babies would be lured away from the faith if they came into contact with Protestant institutions or were adopted by Protestant parents – would remain a defining feature of the work of St Patrick's Guild and other Catholic organizations that interacted with unmarried mothers well into the second half of the twentieth century. In some cases where the faith of the mother or child was perceived to be in jeopardy, Miss Cruice intervened personally. The 1922 report tells the story of 'Case number 484':

> A young Irish woman, un-married, and about to become a mother, went to Liverpool to avoid publicity. While there she happily came under the care of the Catholic Rescue Society, who had mother and baby brought to Dublin and given over to our care. Later on the girl, who was unfortunately in love with a married man, the father of her child, made an attempt to leave the country in his company. Providence intervened on her behalf, and her plans became known to the Guild in the most extraordinary manner. Miss Cruice was able to intercept the passage booked to leave the country, and the girl's Parish Priest was being communicated with, immediate action was taken and her plans frustrated. She was made to see the gravity of her situation, and is now doing well. She is, of course, kept under close observation.

This culture of surveillance and control allowed St Patrick's Guild to 'assist mothers whose previous characters give promise of redemption, and whose religion might be in danger if timely help were not forthcoming, and to secure the baptism of infants, and induce parents to approach the sacraments'. Offering an assurance of 'absolute privacy to the girl' was paramount to protecting her faith, wrote Miss Cruice, for 'privacy is the chief bait by which Proselytizing Homes attract their victims'. The pledge to find and monitor good homes for the children – 'to board out children with respectable families, and to visit such children from time to time' – ranked far below the primary objective of protecting the religious faith of mother and child.

In February 2011 I came across this neatly typed report among several old manila files marked 'SPG' in the archives of the Archdiocese of Dublin, a high-ceilinged room adorned with crucifixes and large windows on an upper floor of Clonliffe College in Drumcondra, a short walk from the Archbishop's palace. Once the place where Dublin's priests were trained, the sprawling seminary had been shuttered for the past decade owing to a lack of vocations, and on the day that I visited the campus had an eerie, empty feel, the vast grounds bleak and bare, the enormous car park nearly vacant. Now repurposed as the administrative centre for the Archdiocese of Dublin, the building had become a repository for many of the secrets of the Catholic Church. I had driven past the iron gates of Clonliffe College countless times growing up in Dublin, but my visit that week – a few days after I had sat down with my family to interview them – was the first time I had ever ventured inside. The entrance hall, all shiny oak doors and buffed tile floors, gave off the odour of beeswax polish that I associated with childhood weekends spent visiting the enclosed convent where we saw Mam's distant cousin, the doleful and diabetic Mother Ursula, and the hospice run by the Sisters of Charity in Harold's Cross, where my grandfather had lived out his final years in a persistent vegetative state.

I had expected resistance from the archdiocese to my request to spend time exploring the archives. Not quite two years had passed since the publication of the Ryan Report, the product of the state's decade-long investigation into widespread and horrific child abuse in residential institutions managed by Catholic religious orders. Although the Archbishop of Dublin, Diarmuid Martin, was, unlike his predecessors and many of his fellow prelates, supporting research-driven investigations of the Church's involvement in institutional abuse, I assumed that an email from a journalist adoptee would set off alarm bells. But I received a friendly reply from the archivist, who promised to schedule me in for a day's sleuthing. 'I suggest you bring a digital camera,' she wrote. 'That way you can photograph as much as possible and read it at a later stage.'

Buoyed by this warm response, I arrived at the archives at 9.30 on the appointed morning armed with my digital camera, reporter's notebook and pen. The archivist, knowing I was interested in adoption, had already prepared some files, ushering me to a desk beneath a large window where a lidded cardboard box and several manila folders stood neatly stacked. The long room, divided in half by a narrow corridor flanked on either side by rows and rows of shelves, reminded me of many happy hours spent as an undergraduate leafing through original source material in the National Archives. Now, noting the size of the box marked 'Byrne Papers' in black pen – the personal documents of Archbishop Edward Joseph Byrne, who ruled the diocese of Dublin from 1921 to 1940 – I realized that I had my work cut out for me. I placed my bag on the seat, lifted the lid off the box and peered inside.

In the first years of independence, Ireland's new leaders were focused primarily on shoring up the legitimacy of the fledgling state, restoring law and order, and reconstructing the country's infrastructure. But this turbulent time also offered an opportunity for the state – and the Church – to reassert moral order. Between 1921 and 1927, figures showed a 29 per cent increase in the number of births outside of marriage, a source of embarrassment to the state and a challenge to the notion of Ireland as a Catholic bastion. In 1927, in one of the first inquiries following independence into the issue of the unmarried mother and her child, the *Report of the Commission on the Relief of the Sick and Destitute Poor* stated, 'Our belief is that with returning stability of government and the gradual tightening of the reins of discipline, both governmental and parental, that we may look forward to a decrease in the numbers of these births.' A girl or woman who became pregnant out of wedlock was immediately disadvantaged in a number of ways. She might find it impossible to access – or be forced to leave – education or work; living independently as a single mother was, for many, simply impossible. If she felt unable to turn to her family, she might find herself at the mercy of a residential institution; often, girls were brought to such institutions *by* their families. In the early years of independent Ireland, many such women ended up in the 'county home', part of the state's network of poor-relief institutions that long pre-dated independence. Other unmarried mothers, especially those 'repeat offenders' with more than one illegitimate child, ended up in Magdalen laundries following the birth of their children in the county homes or elsewhere. The laundries, mostly run by orders of nuns, facilitated the removal from mainstream society of women deemed morally dubious: not just unmarried mothers but also victims of sexual abuse, girls who had grown up in industrial schools but were deemed too immature to enter into society, and women who had committed certain crimes or who had special needs. In de facto detention, many of these women toiled for years in the laundries, which served as a money-making venture for the religious orders who were in many cases operating on lucrative contracts from the state.

Following the publication of the *Report of the Commission on the Relief of the Sick and Destitute Poor* in 1927, Ireland's local authorities turned increasingly to religious orders to help with the mounting problem of the unmarried mother and to lessen the dependence on the county home. This led to the establishment of several mother-and-baby homes across the country. These so-called 'special homes' were operated privately by the religious orders, outside of any system of state regulation, although several did receive local government grants for the women and children in their care. Two other homes – in Pelletstown, Dublin, and Tuam, County Galway – were funded entirely by local government but were run by religious orders.

There was a clear class divide between the 'special homes' and the county homes, the former reserved for 'first-time offenders' and the 'better type of girl'. The county home was reserved for the 'poorest class' and for those deemed morally irredeemable, the 'recidivists' or 'repeat offenders'. Those sent to the 'special homes' had, in the eyes of the Church and Irish society, the greatest chance of rehabilitation.

Most unmarried mothers who gave birth in the mother-and-baby homes were expected to remain in the home for up to two years, during which time they worked to earn their keep and care for their children while arrangements were made to board the children out. Women who had the financial means could pay their way out after a shorter confinement. Many women who could not afford to leave stayed in these homes until their children were old enough to be transferred to an orphanage, industrial school or to be boarded out or, after 1952, placed for adoption.

In 1925 and 1926 the registrar-general reported that the mortality rate among illegitimate children was five times that of legitimate infants, and that one out of three illegitimate infants did not survive the first year of life. The 1933 Hospitals Commission Report documented a 'death-rate of approximately 295 per 1,000 births in 1929 of illegitimate children, compared with 140 and 105 in Northern Ireland and England respectively'. In the mid 1930s, the illegitimate child in Ireland was four times less likely to reach his first birthday than his legitimate counterpart.

The causes of death for these children varied. Some died in the county homes, victims of disease or, in some cases, malnutrition. 'Commissioners take a very serious view of the number of deaths during the week and require a detailed report from Doctor dealing with same,' the Dublin board of health and public assistance wrote in 1926 of the horrendous conditions in the Pelletstown mother-and-baby home. 'It has also been brought to the Commissioners' notice that babies leaving Pelletstown to be placed at nurse often present a delicate and even starved appearance.' In 1924, the Dublin health board condemned Miss Cruice for placing a child in a foster home where two children, previously sent from St Patrick's Guild, had already died. In February 2015, following explosive research by a local historian into the deaths of 796 children at the Tuam mother-and-baby home, the Irish government appointed a special commission to investigate conditions and mortality in Ireland's mother-and-baby homes between 1922 and 1998.

Some illegitimate babies died through concealment or abandonment, left alone by their desperate mothers to succumb to the elements in a lonely field or hedgerow. Others were dispatched to the care of reluctant relatives only to suffer a slow and painful death through neglect. In a heart-rending passage in her memoir *Are You Somebody?*, Nuala O'Faolain recounted an incident during her north Dublin childhood in the 1950s when the domestic maid in her family home

> fell to the floor and gave birth to a baby. It transpired that the butcher, when he called with the meat, had been having sex with her. The baby went to the maid's mother. My mother happened to call on that house a few weeks later. The baby was emaciated, immobile, sinking into death. 'Sure, who wants it?' the grandmother said.

Although Ireland modernized economically as the century progressed, attitudes to single mothers and their children remained stuck in the mode articulated by Miss Cruice in 1922, and the network of mother-and-baby homes and Magdalen laundries was still very much intact in the early 1970s, when Sarah became pregnant and when Mary and Liam set out to adopt a child. In May 1943 Miss Cruice handed control of St Patrick's Guild over to the Irish Sisters of Charity, a congregation that also operated Magdalen laundries in Dublin and Cork and industrial schools for girls in various locations across the country. A report written by the sisters two months later detailed discussions about whether St Patrick's Guild should continue to serve Miss Cruice's 'better class of girl' or offer its services more widely.

> Should there be a ruling regarding cases of the married woman whose husband is not aware – who is at the War – or gone to England, etc.? Should there be a ruling regarding 2nd offenders or should all these cases be left – after careful examination – to the discernment of the person in charge?

(NB This might be the more sensible method. In some cases appeals have been made from Priests in the Country regarding cases, intimating to us the absolute necessity of secrecy – i.e. where a relation of a Priest or Nun is concerned.)

The report concluded, 'The <u>mixing</u> of cases, i.e. 1st and 2nd offenders, seems very harmful. It has the effect of lessening the gravity of sin.'

Excellent archival research by Mike Milotte for his 1997 book *Banished Babies* paints a useful picture of St Patrick's Guild in the decades leading up to my adoption. The Guild was still orientated towards the 'better class of girl'. 'These unfortunate girls are of good class with, usually, excellent background,' Sister Frances Elizabeth wrote in a letter to the office of an Irish government minister in 1952, which was also the year in which legislation was finally passed creating a legal framework for adoption. 'In most cases it is imperative that they return to their employment within a fortnight, or less, after the birth. Many of them are working in such places as government offices, solicitors' offices and commercial offices, schools or hospitals.' As would be the case two decades later when Sarah approached the Guild for assistance, secrecy was paramount. 'In such circumstances,' Sister Frances Elizabeth wrote, 'the greatest secrecy is not merely desirable but essential. Should there be a shadow of suspicion or scandal the girl's whole future might be in jeopardy.' Between 1947 and 1967, according to its own figures, St Patrick's Guild sent 572 children to the United States for adoption, the largest number of any adoption agency in the state.

On Friday, 18 February 1972, Liam took a day off work and drove Mary to Number 50, Middle Abbey Street, a red-brick Georgian house opposite the back entrance to

Arnotts department store. It was to be their first interview with St Patrick's Guild. I now have a record of that interview, taken from my adoption file. Many times following my reunion with Sarah, I had requested access to my file, but my polite enquiries met with steely resistance from the Guild. I was desperate to peek inside this file, curious to know whether there were any personal documents – letters, details about Sarah's pregnancy or my birth – that might help me plump out the narrative of the earliest days of my life. The agency's reluctance to hand over this information maddened me. The details within my file were of interest only to me – and of no harm to anyone else – yet I was made to feel guilty for asking.

Even though Sarah had no objection to St Patrick's Guild granting access to my file, and had told them so in person, the law was not on my side. I was one of 60,000 Irish adoptees with no statutory rights to my birth records, including my adoption file and birth certificate. Those rights had long existed for adoptees elsewhere: in Scotland since 1930, in England and Wales since 1976 and in Northern Ireland since 1987. But in Ireland, all adoptions were 'closed' adoptions: adopted people had no legal right to know who their biological parents were and birth parents had no legal right to trace children surrendered for adoption. A 1998 Supreme Court ruling upheld this position.

In August 2014, frustrated by the continued stonewalling of St Patrick's Guild, I plucked up the courage and requested a meeting. Several years earlier, the organization had moved away from Haddington Road and into a new office situated on a large gated campus of religious buildings on Merrion Road. On the morning of the meeting I stopped at a petrol station and bought a box of chocolates – a gift for the nun that I was about to meet. A little further down the street, at the gates of the building, I paused beneath the awning of a bus stop and reached into my handbag to extract a pair of black high-heeled shoes, quickly exchanging them for the ballet flats on my feet. It felt ludicrous, but I was nervous about what was to come and looking for courage in any form. I thought a little bit of height might do me good.

Twenty minutes later I was sitting opposite the nun who had interviewed me fifteen years before at the start of my search for Sarah. We were the only people in the room. On the table in front of us was a tray of tea and biscuits. The air was thick with tension. When I casually mentioned to the nun that I worked as a journalist, she replied, 'Well, I certainly don't want to read anything about this in a newspaper article, or anything like that.'

I limped on, outlining the purpose of my visit: to request access to my adoption file.

'We would give the information if it was there,' she said, 'but we don't have that information.'

A long, painful silence filled the air. The nun's steely gaze was making my heart race, but I continued to press. Perhaps there might still be files relating to my time at the baby home where I had lived for six weeks shortly after my birth? Feeding schedules, records like that? The nun sighed heavily. 'I don't know what's there from Temple Hill. I would have assumed that you would have got all of that from Catherine before. We would have to go through the whole of it and it's not likely to happen any time in the near future.'

Thirty minutes later I left the building empty-handed. The nun had ended our meeting with a vague promise that 'it might be possible' for St Patrick's Guild to release some information from my file – when time and resources allowed – but I wasn't holding out any great hope. I walked away from St Patrick's Guild imagining a room filled with dusty files, wondering just how difficult it would be to extract mine, remembering the Srebrenica hospital raid.

For months I heard nothing. Finally, in late 2014, I asked Dad to write a polite but pointed letter, reiterating my request and stating categorically that he and Mam had no objections. Dad's letter seemed to do the trick. Six months later an envelope arrived at Number 49, brimming with photocopied pages relating to Liam and Mary's request to adopt. Accompanying the contents of my file was a cover letter to my father, signed by a nun whose name I did not recognize.

Dear Mr Palmer,

Enclosed please find copies of the information we have on the record for you and your wife Mary. It is up to you what you wish to share with Caitríona.

The last line felt like a kick in the teeth. The nuns at St Patrick's Guild were still regarding me as a non-entity.

Neither Liam nor Mary can recollect much from that first interview at St Patrick's Guild other than a desperation to please the nun in charge and to contain their nerves. The account I have from that morning, under the heading 'Prospective Adopters', records their names, their address, their ages and occupations. Under the heading 'Husband', a Sister Angela records Liam's physical attributes – 'Height: 5' 6", Hair: Brown, Eyes: Blue'. Under the heading 'General Impression', she notes that Liam is 'Very Nice' and Mary 'Very nice and outgoing'. A quarter of the interview is devoted to Mary's reproductive health, including the name and address of her doctor. 'Had a rupture last September,' Sister Angela notes, and then, underlined, 'most likely never to conceive again'. Under 'Comments' there is the observation that 'Mrs Palmer has never used any form of contraceptives other than <u>Safe Period</u>' – a nod to the Archbishop of Dublin John Charles McQuaid's insistence that proof be issued demonstrating that prospective adopters were not 'shirking' natural parenthood.

Following this interview, Mary and Liam submitted their official application to St Patrick's Guild, a four-page document, written in Liam's distinguished hand. It is a moving insight into their life at the time. The application notes Liam's occupation as 'Clerical Officer – British Rail'. Asked to describe their home, Liam writes, '3 Bedrooms, Sitting room, Dining room, Large Kitchen'. Asked to state the age and sex of the child that they wish to adopt, Liam notes, 'GIRL. BABY – under 1 year'. There is no hesitation in the answers for Question 11, 'Are you both practising Roman Catholics?' In the boxes marked 'Husband' and 'Wife', Liam has written 'Yes' and 'Yes'. On the final page of the application is a crude map of our estate, drawn in my father's hand, with an X marking our house.

The process was gaining momentum. Three days later Mary took a train into town to visit the office of her gynaecologist, Dr Patrick O'Grady, on the salubrious Wellington Road. 'I went to him to tell him that we would adopt,' Mam told me that February evening in Thérèse's dining room. 'He listened and confirmed to me that I couldn't have any more children.' Several hours later Mary returned to Number 49 with a typed letter from Dr O'Grady addressed to St Patrick's Guild.

Dear Sister,

Re. above patient who has a very bad obstetrical history. She had a miscarriage in May, 1969, and an ectopic pregnancy in September, 1971. She was very ill post-operatively. I think it would be dangerous

for her to have another pregnancy, as it would probably end up as an
ectopic. I recommend her strongly for adoption.

Yours sincerely,
P. J. O'Grady

'It was Thérèse who wanted a little girl,' Mam told me that February evening in 2011. '"Am I going to get my little sister?" That's all you kept saying,' she said, nodding across at Thérèse. 'We applied the end of February, and you arrived in early June. The nuns from St Patrick's Guild came out and they went through everything.'

'Hang on,' I said, interrupting as I did a quick mental calculation in my head. 'That was very fast.'

'It was a friend of Aunty Kathleen's, Sister Brendan, who was a nun in the hospice. She rang Sister Angela who was in charge of St Patrick's Guild and that was how we got you so quick.'

Sister Angela: a name I had heard invoked frequently – and with fear – as a child. 'What was she like?' I asked Mam.

'She was all right, I suppose. She was a small little nun, kind. But like all the nuns back then she was bloody strict. I suppose she had to be careful. She was putting a baby into a home and she didn't know us. I suppose everything had to be A-1 for her.'

'Did you have to hand over financial details?'

'Everything,' said Mam, taking a sip of her tea. 'And when they came to visit the house, they went through everything, through every single corner of our house. They went from room to room, looking through wardrobes and everything.'

Growing up, I had often heard stories about the 'spot-check' visits to Number 49 – the phone call out of the blue from Sister Angela to say that she was on the way, the frantic scurrying by Mary to rearrange our already tidy house. Once inside, Sister Angela's routine was usually the same: passing pleasantries with the Palmers, a cup of tea and then a request to inspect the house. Sometimes she would glide through the downstairs living rooms, other times she would ask to see upstairs. Once, much to my mother's surprise, she asked to look inside the hot press.

Often throughout my young adulthood, my mother would recount these stories about Sister Angela with comic effect, but behind the laughter was genuine fear. This tiny nun wielded real power: the ability to wave a magic wand and vanquish a family's sorrow by giving them a child, and the power to take that child back.

Tidiness and cleanliness: Spotless.
Distance from church and school: Both near.
Motives of adoptive parents: 'We would like more children.'

These are the notations from a spot check during that first year, the very last document included in the papers St Patrick's Guild sent to my parents in the spring of 2015.

Relationship with their children: Very good.
Relationship one towards the other: Excellent.
Their attitude towards education: Very sound.

'They checked Garda records,' Mam told me. 'They went to doctors. They went to Larry Forrestal, who was our parish priest at the time. You had to give all your details: who you are, what you had, what your background was, your parents, where you worked.'

I was writing furiously, taking notes. My mother paused. I looked up. She was smiling and looking across at Dad.

'But there was great jubilation in our house, wasn't there, Liam, when Caitríona arrived?'

Dad looked up. He had been fingering a knot of wood in the dining-room table as he listened to Mam. He smiled, looking directly at me.

'There was great jubilation,' he said. 'Great jubilation indeed.'

8

In the summer of 2000, still fragile following my bicycle accident, I crossed the Atlantic with Dan to attend the wedding of a close friend of his in Rhode Island. We spent a couple of days in Boston, sightseeing and meeting up with old friends. The day before we left to drive to the wedding, Dan, unusually jittery and pensive, suggested that we take a walk across Boston Common. I was in no mood to traipse about in the muggy midday heat, but I reluctantly agreed when Dan continued to press. Halfway across the Common, near an enormous craggy oak, he stopped, pulled me beneath the leafy expanse, got down on one knee and asked if I would marry him.

The following summer Dan and I were in Dublin for our wedding. By then, Sarah was relaxed enough in my company to agree to my tentative suggestion that we abandon the dark corners of the Westbury bar and venture further afield, and Dan joined us for lunch at a small Italian restaurant in the city centre. It felt like a watershed moment. I had a sense that Sarah had finally come out into the light, where she was obliged to interact with a friendly waitress and to sit in close quarters with other patrons. Dan took a photograph of the two of us as we lingered over dessert and coffee. The photo is one of the very few that I have of Sarah and me together and it is easily my favourite. We look intimate and happy, relaxed in each other's presence, our heads touching gently as we lean together. Many times I have thought to frame this photograph, but I have resisted the urge. With our relationship still underground, it has never felt right. Instead, I keep the photo in a leather-bound album in a box beneath my bed, waiting for the day when I can finally unearth Sarah and bring her into the light.

Another time that summer, we arranged to meet outside the Dart station in Howth. We'd never met out in the open, and Sarah looked exposed and fearful as I approached. Howth was a risky choice – we each had many friends and relatives who might turn up there. But I was sick and tired of hiding indoors and desperate to bring some semblance of normalcy to the relationship. I thought a bit of fresh air would do us both good.

'One day I'll tell everyone,' Sarah told me that afternoon as we sat on a low harbour wall watching the yachts bob in the breeze. 'It is right here,' she said, tapping the base of her delicate throat as if to show the precise location where the secret lay festering. 'It's right here and one day it will come out. It will. I promise.'

But there was always a reason to keep it inside, always a plea for more time. *Once the kids are older*, she'd say, *then I'll tell. When they've left school. When my youngest goes to college. When they've all left home.* Paralysed by my inability to confront Sarah, to confess how demeaning it was to be kept hidden, I acquiesced to her terms. Sometimes I have wondered whether, if Sarah understood the true extent of my pain, she would tell her family about me. I'll never know for sure, but I suspect not. The power of the secret was too great.

On Bloomsday – 16 June 2001 – Dan and I were married amongst friends and family in a tiny blue wooden church in the foothills of the Dublin Mountains. After the ceremony we drove through the winding country lanes to a Palladian mansion overlooking the purple and yellow expanse of the

Great Sugar Loaf mountain. We drank Pimm's and champagne, strolled through the magnificent gardens and, after dinner, danced the night away to the music of a gypsy folk band. I was deliriously happy, full of gratitude and surrounded by all the people I loved – everyone, that is, except Sarah. I had invited her to the wedding, assuring her that she would be welcomed by everyone. Mam asked me to convey that she would love to see her at the wedding, even if it meant just coming briefly to the service before slipping away. But Sarah, who had not met either Liam or Mary, politely demurred. I found my mind wandering several times that day, wondering how she was, what she was doing, whether she was thinking of me.

A couple of weeks previously, on a brief weekend visit to Dublin from London, where Dan and I were now living, I asked Sarah to meet me in the basement of a graceful Georgian house on Upper Mount Street. It was my final wedding-dress fitting and at Mam's suggestion I had asked Sarah to come along. It seemed like a way of including her in my wedding and I was pleased when she agreed. Looking back, I am amazed by my mother's magnanimity in that moment, to step aside and allow this other woman to take her place. Intuitively, Mam knew that I would be anxious to include Sarah but would be too afraid to ask. Suggesting that Sarah accompany me that day was an act of unbridled generosity, of pure maternal love.

On the appointed day Sarah was a few minutes late, leaving me enough time to explain to the seamstress our complicated relationship. I was anxious to avoid any awkward questions. Fifteen minutes later Sarah sat on a couch while I stood before her, wearing the simple long-sleeved fitted silk ivory gown that I had chosen to wear up the aisle. She was visibly moved, praising the cut, my silhouette and how happy I seemed. But there was also an air of unease and distance about her, a disconcerting evasiveness. As we said goodbye, Sarah pushed into my hands an envelope containing a wedding card stuffed with a large wad of cash. It would be the last time that we would see each other before the wedding and, for the first time in her presence, I felt clingy as we said goodbye.

An hour later, unsettled and distracted, I returned home to Number 49 on the train, trying to make sense of Sarah's mood, disappointed that the moment had fallen flat. Perhaps asking Sarah to play mother-of-the-bride for a few minutes was too much for her to bear? I was annoyed at myself for my clumsiness, for my lack of tact. At the same time I resented the weight and potency of the secret and the shadow it cast over my interactions with Sarah, making me second-guess my every move. As the doors of the train slid open at Raheny station I stepped on to the platform preoccupied by one looping thought: *How much longer can this go on?*

The following day I returned to the bridal designer, this time with Mam in tow. I had made both appointments weeks earlier, knowing that the final mother–daughter moment, by right, belonged to Mam and that she should be the person by my side when I left the bridal shop with the wedding gown in hand. In a bid for total transparency, I had told Sarah that I would be returning the following day with Mam. Both women were exceedingly gracious about these bizarre machinations. But I was exhausted by the emotional ping-pong of ensuring that both mothers in my life felt indispensable, recognized and loved.

In the autumn of 2002, Dan accepted an offer from the *Guardian* to become the paper's stringer in Tehran. We broke the news to Liam and Mary that October on a flying weekend visit to Dublin, sitting beneath the picture of the Sacred Heart in the kitchen of Number 49 while nervously fingering cups of tea.

'You two need a brain scan,' Mam said, breaking the uncomfortable silence that had settled over the kitchen table after Dan delivered the news. 'I don't know why in God's name you want to go to those kinds of places. Can't you just stay where you are in London?'

We travelled two months later. I had read all the travel guides and acquired the uniform that I believed best suited a foreign woman living in the Islamic Republic. As we entered Iranian airspace I made my way to the toilets at the back of the plane, emerging moments later in an oversized Marks & Spencer black mackintosh and polyester scarf, my face scrubbed entirely free of make-up. I had never felt dowdier. An hour later I stood in shock in the arrivals hall at Mehrabad airport as I watched Iranian women teetering past on outrageously high heels and in tightly fitted mid-length coats that left little to the imagination. Their faces were coated in layers of foundation, their hair barely covered by diaphanous hijabs. As we settled in Tehran, I quickly adjusted my own wardrobe.

Dan and I were living in north Tehran, in a large two-bedroomed apartment on a busy shop-lined street. Every morning we made coffee and stood together at the French windows in our living room to admire the snow-capped expanse of the Alborz mountain range that stretched behind the city. By noon, the mountains would be invisible, blanketed in a choking smog. Feeling adrift without the rhythms of regular work, I moped about Tehran for the first couple of months. Every day I travelled north up Shariati Street in a shared taxi to a language school where I sat in a dreary classroom and did my best to learn Farsi, the complex but beautiful language of the Persians. Free in the afternoon, I would wander down Valiasr Street, the immense sycamore-lined boulevard built by the Shah in the glory days of the Pahlavi monarchy to rival the avenues of Paris. There, I would work up the courage to sit in a cafe and order rose water or pistachio ice cream. More often than not I would take a taxi home, stopping at the bustling vegetable market at the end of our street where I would cause a scene amongst the other customers with my fumbled attempts to buy plump aubergines, courgettes and furry almonds still in their pods. Back at home, preparing dinner, I would try to replicate Iran's delicate rice dishes, pairing the food with a glass of vinegary home-brewed wine that our Armenian alcohol dealer smuggled into our apartment every couple of weeks in a black refuse bag in exchange for an outrageous sum of cash. Other nights Dan and I would head out to meet our widening circle of expat and Iranian friends.

By the summer I was becoming bored with life as an expat housewife. Frustrated by the Iranian authorities' refusal to allow me to pursue a humanitarian-focused career, I decided to reinvent myself as a journalist. This would enable me to join Dan on his reporting assignments across Iran and hopefully, with the American-led invasion raging next door, into Iraq. There were no other Irish journalists resident in Tehran, and it wasn't long before I got my first big story in the *Irish Times* when a hapless Irish citizen was kidnapped by armed bandits while cycling across the country.

For Sarah, my reincarnation as a journalist added a new dimension to our relationship. By buying a copy of a newspaper containing one of my stories, Sarah was finally able to bring me into her home, to open the page to my report and read it in full view of her husband and family. Occasionally she could tune in to Irish radio and listen as my voice filled the narrow kitchen of her house. Sarah began to collect my newspaper clippings, storing them next to my letters in the locker that she used in the teachers' lounge of the school where she taught. Sometimes, during lunch and tea breaks, she would take them out, allowing her eyes to drift over my name and picture byline. As the years progressed, I often wondered whether Sarah had more of a tangible relationship to the Caitríona Palmer in the newspaper than to the woman who met her clandestinely a few times a year on visits to Dublin, or whom she occasionally phoned. (In the years to come, as technology improved, Sarah would quit making excuses to slip out of her house to call me from a payphone down the street – frantically feeding in coin after coin – and instead sent cheery texts from her mobile phone.)

In October 2003, we agreed, for old time's sake, to meet each other at the Westbury for tea. At some point during that meeting Sarah began to sink low in her seat, placing her right hand over her forehead as though shielding her eyes from a blinding ray of light. It was clear that there was somebody in the room who she knew, that she was trying to make herself invisible. I suggested that we move. Sarah shook her head but continued to slouch, her eyes darting across the room, her entire demeanour oozing fear and apprehension until her acquaintance left and Sarah, visibly relieved, sat up straight in her chair.

For me, keeping our relationship under wraps was much easier. I'd already coached bemused friends and relatives on what to do should they ever run into me in the company of an older woman: smile, say hello and keep walking. But the nature of my relationship with Sarah was hard for them to comprehend. 'She hasn't told anyone about you?' was the first thing friends and acquaintances asked when I mentioned the secret affair. 'How come? What is she afraid of?' I prattled off a list of standard replies. She's worried that she'll lose her family, I told them. She's scared and traumatized. She's still haunted by the stigma and shame that she endured during the pregnancy. It's easier for her to keep everything under wraps. My friends, at least those who were versed in the peculiarities of Catholic Ireland, mostly understood Sarah's predicament, even if its implications for our relationship were hard to absorb.

By the close of that year I had come to detest the power imbalance in our relationship, seeing myself as the cause of Sarah's shame and paranoia, her sadness and regret. I hated being invisible to her husband, evidently a good man who adored her, and to her three children, half-siblings that I longed to meet. I felt Sarah had duped me when she said, early on in our relationship, that she would spill the beans once she had come to terms with the reality of my being back in her life. Never did I expect that one year would turn into five, and five years into ten, and ten into fifteen. Surely I was special enough not to be kept in the shadows for ever? Surely her love for me was stronger than her fear? And so I kept waiting for the day when she would summon the courage to gather her beloved husband and children around her and say, 'I had another child once, a long time ago. I gave her away but now she has come back. I think she is lovely and I would like you to meet her.'

Dan and I were elated when, in April 2004, we discovered that I was pregnant with our first child. Just weeks earlier we had celebrated Sizdah Bedar, the thirteenth day of Nowruz, the vernal equinox, with Iranian friends at a large country house outside Tehran. The day was unusually warm and the air smelt of the fresh damp earth of the burgeoning spring.

We sat outside on our friend's veranda and drank home-brewed wine and ate steaming bowls of *ash-e-reshteh*, a thick and velvety Persian soup made of noodles and beans that is meant to usher in good luck for the year ahead. Later we strolled through a dense thicket of mulberry and cedar trees, ripe with tiny green buds, to a wide and shallow river that bordered the property. We stood on the riverbank and tossed luminously green clumps of *sabze*, wheatgrass, into the fast-moving water, a tradition meant to banish negativity from our lives. My Iranian friends showed me first how to make a wish by tying a knot in the tall grass. Not yet aware of the tiny new life taking hold inside my body, I knotted my grass and wished for a baby, casting the *sabze* far into the expanse of the iridescent flow.

A few weeks later our life in Iran came to an abrupt halt. A phone call from an official in the Ministry of Culture and Islamic Guidance informed Dan that his journalist visa was being revoked and that he had a week to leave the country.

We knew why this was happening. Several weeks earlier we had requested permission from the Iranian authorities to travel to Bam, an ancient city in southern Iran that had been levelled months before by an earthquake measuring 6.6 on the Richter scale. Asleep in their beds when the quake struck in the early hours of 26 December, nearly half of Bam's residents – over 26,000 people – had been killed. The city's clay citadel, a perfectly preserved adobe structure dating from 500 BC, was razed to the ground.

The authorities were polite but firm: we could travel to Bam but we were not to report on what we saw there. We decided to go, accepting an offer from an enterprising Iranian friend to volunteer as aid workers at his father's charity, clearing rubble from the pathways and distributing food from tent to tent. Once we were there, it became clear why the authorities were so keen to keep us out. Three months following the earthquake, the reconstruction efforts were plagued by mismanagement and corruption. Thousands of hungry families still lived in tents by the side of the road, the interiors infested with flies and filled with the stench from the open latrines nearby. Appalled by what we saw, Dan and I wrote reports for the *Guardian* and the *Irish Times* respectively, criticizing the government's relief efforts. Two days after his Bam piece appeared, the *Observer* published another article by Dan recounting the torture that the student activist Ahmad Batebi – sentenced to death for being photographed holding aloft the bloodied T-shirt of a friend injured during student protests – had suffered in jail. Two critical articles in such quick succession was too much for the regime. We pleaded with the ministry to revoke Dan's expulsion, but the decision was final. On 10 May, after a lively and emotional late-night party hosted by diplomatic friends, we caught an early-morning flight out of Tehran for the last time.

Our next stop was Washington, DC, where we felt there were good prospects for steady work in our fields; also, in DC we'd be roughly midway between Dan's family in California and mine in Dublin. By the autumn of 2004 we were happily ensconced in an apartment in a narrow Victorian brownstone house. On 21 November, Liam, our son, surprised us by arriving two weeks early, a Thanksgiving baby with a downy crown of ginger-brown hair and a cascade of long arms and legs. Holding Liam and scanning his tiny face in the immediate aftermath of his birth, I felt a lightning flash of recognition, an arousal in my senses that at first was difficult to place. Moments later it hit me: Liam looked a *lot* like Sarah, particularly across the eyes and in the endearing way that he furrowed his puzzled newborn brow.

In the space of five years, I had welcomed two new blood

relatives into my life, a biological bonus that felt a lot like winning the lottery. Living in such close proximity to my own flesh and blood was an intoxicating novelty and I could not get enough of Liam. I held him constantly, burrowing my face in the delicious, doughy folds of his skin. I passed those first few months of motherhood in a blissful trance, high on the love hormone oxytocin and the exhilaration of seeing my own DNA reflected up close.

As I held and nursed Liam over the following weeks, I found my mind constantly filled with thoughts of Sarah. Now that I had my own child I understood, in magnified clarity, the anguish of the decision that she had faced thirty-two years before.

9

Thinking about Sarah, during my own first weeks of motherhood, my moods flitted between overwhelming pity for her and something that felt like anger. Intellectually, I had always understood the societal forces that had caused Sarah to surrender me for adoption; but now, holding my own child, I could not understand how she could have given me up. If someone had come to take Liam from me, I would have fought them to the death. Hadn't Sarah felt the same?

For the first time in my life, with Liam as my muse, I began to visualize myself as a baby. I noticed, with amazement, how Liam instantly stopped crying the moment I – not Dan or anyone else – picked him up. Having never dared venture there before, I imagined myself in the hours after my birth, nuzzling into Sarah, her voice a familiar and comforting beacon in my newborn haze. I envisaged what it was like to inhale her scent, to continue to hear – on 19 April, the 20th and the morning of the 21st – the heartbeat that had lulled me to sleep in the womb. Then I imagined what it was like, sometime late in the day on 21 April 1972, to wake up alone and hungry, to cry for Sarah but to feel instead the starched white cotton and inhale the unfamiliar scent of whatever maternity ward nurse picked me up. *Where is my mother? I want my mother.*

Liam's birth also aroused within me a sense of betrayal that I had tiptoed around ever since my reunion with Sarah five years earlier. In the last few weeks of my pregnancy, I had hoped that the birth of Sarah's first grandchild would somehow prompt her to acknowledge my existence to her family. If I wasn't special enough to be shouted from the rooftops then surely Liam – who, as the days and weeks passed, resembled his biological grandmother more and more – would do the trick? Imagining Sarah's delight in meeting her grandchild, I took Liam back to Ireland just five weeks after his birth, baptizing him in the local church in Raheny, surrounded by friends and family. After a respectable amount of time at Number 49, I asked Dad one morning to drive me to the Marine Hotel in Sutton, where, shaking with emotion, I gently placed Liam in Sarah's arms. I watched with delight and hope as she deliriously drank him in. But despite Sarah's joy at meeting her grandson, she gave no indication that anything would change.

Haunted by a creeping sense of outrage, and frustrated that Liam's birth had not, as I had hoped, changed the direction of my relationship with Sarah, I began to wonder about other people in my shoes – secret sons and daughters. One afternoon in the spring of 2005, while Liam took a nap, I began to poke around adoption-support websites. I emailed a friend, an Irish academic in the US who was researching Ireland's troubled history with unmarried mothers. He provided some leads. I called Catherine in Dublin to ask whether she knew of other cases like mine. Countless, she told me. Over time, stories began to trickle into my inbox: other Irish adoptees who had tracked down their biological parents only to be told that they were to remain in the shadows. Through an adoption charity in Dublin I learned about a young woman, a successful professional, who had discovered to her joy that her birth mother had gone on to marry her biological father and that she had four full – and blissfully unaware – siblings. And yet her birth parents, when contacted by the agency that had handled their child's adoption, refused to meet with her. 'We don't want you in our life,' they said via an emissary.

'Please respect our privacy.' Another adoptee, a young woman in the west of Ireland, tracked down her birth mother, who reluctantly agreed to meet with her in a hotel bar near her home town. Skittish and cold, afraid to look her daughter in the eye, this terrified woman begged her not to contact her again. 'I will meet you this once but never again. I don't want anything to do with you,' she told her. 'Nobody knows about your existence. It has to remain like that.'

These stories both horrified and, in a strange way, reassured me. While my relationship with Sarah was complicated, at least I had her in my life and I knew that she loved me. But what were all these mothers afraid of in a country that was no longer in thrall to the Catholic Church? What could have been said or done to silence them for ever?

In January 2006, I emailed a contact at RTÉ, Ireland's national broadcaster, to pitch a radio documentary exploring the phenomenon of Ireland's secret birth mothers. I imagined the airwaves echoing with the voices of women like Sarah, telling the stories – most likely for the first time – of their hidden pregnancies and why they felt compelled to keep their children a secret. An enthusiastic producer commissioned the piece. I began to do research, finding a charity in Ireland that held regular meetings for birth mothers who had relinquished children to adoption decades before. The director of the charity agreed to circulate my details to the group. A number of women called me. But every time I requested that they record their stories for national radio, I met with steely resistance. By the spring of 2006, without a single woman committed to sharing her story on air, I was forced to abandon the project.

That's when the kernel for this book first took root, one night in the quiet of my bedroom in April 2006, while I nursed Liam to sleep. Perhaps I was the person who could break the silence and shed light on the origins of all this shame by exploring Sarah's story and telling of our peculiar relationship? All of a sudden, I knew that I needed to write a book, to relay the story and – more importantly – to make sense out of the confusion and the pain.

In the darkness, with Liam in my arms, I outlined the narrative in my mind. If I looked hard enough at Sarah's past, surely I could work out why she was denying me a place in her life? The history books on my bedside table suggested that the answer lay in Ireland's unconscionable treatment of unmarried mothers, but was it really all the fault of the nuns and priests and Irish society? Perhaps if I could morph from a secret daughter into a probing journalist, the answer would find its way to me? Whatever I discovered, I reasoned, could not be any worse than the pain – the unresolved grief and shame – of being kept hidden away.

On a winter morning in February 2007, a steaming mug of coffee at hand and Liam playing quietly in the corner, I sat at the dining-room table in our apartment in Washington and opened my laptop to check email. I noticed a message with an unfamiliar address under the subject heading 'hi'. Squinting at the screen more closely, my heart skipped a beat. The email appeared to be from Sarah.

Up until then, my written communication with Sarah had been conducted entirely through Catherine and St Patrick's Guild. What had started initially as a deluge of letters had, over the years, dwindled to just a trickle. There were also occasional text messages and hurried phone calls. Now, Sarah had opened a new channel.

Greetings from Dublin. My first email. Hope you are all in great form. Lots of love, Sarah. Xxx

The previous month, I had flown to Dublin with Liam, a belated Christmas visit. One afternoon, the weak January daylight fading across Dublin Bay, I met Sarah at the Marine Hotel. We sat in a corner of the bar and ordered a late lunch, delighting in Liam perched next to us in a booster seat, eagerly scarfing chips. The mood was light and celebratory, despite the winter chill, and I was happy to see Sarah. Happy, too, to observe her watching Liam as he lurched about the hotel in all of his toddler vivacity, full of curiosity and the mischief that being two years old brings.

I had come to the meeting on a mission. The previous year, spooked by the way Liam's arrival had caused a shift in my feelings towards Sarah, I had begun, for the first time in my life, to see a therapist. As Liam grew before my eyes and Sarah's secret remained intact, I was aware of building pressure and understood intuitively that I needed some means to release it. And so, every Tuesday afternoon for the previous couple of months, I had sat in the quiet of a therapist's office in Dupont Circle, ruminating on my past and the bizarre reality of being denied a place in the life of my own birth mother.

Therapy was helpful. It allowed me to sort through my jumble of conflicting emotions and gave me an opportunity to vent my frustrations. I was painfully aware that I had always tiptoed around Sarah, frightened by her emotional fragility and stymied by the artful way she dodged uncomfortable topics. Our conversations were friendly and fun but endlessly frustrating: I had long stopped bringing up the past – including the elephant in the room, my birth father – and never once allowed myself to express to Sarah just how painful it was to be kept a secret.

Emboldened by a burgeoning sense of injustice at how unbalanced the relationship had become, I was determined to make a change. I told my therapist that on this visit to Dublin I would screw up my courage and ask Sarah to engage with me in a more honest way. I would suggest that we find some way to communicate other than the sporadic and rushed calls to my mobile phone that left me feeling depleted and used. I would finally confess to her how truly painful it was to be kept in the shadows. Most importantly, I would ask Sarah to commit – after years of rebuffing my gentle suggestions – to seek therapy for herself. Over the years I had seen her physical posture change worryingly, and I think anyone looking at her would have been able to sense her sadness. In my darkest moments, I felt worried for her life.

That day at the Marine Hotel, Sarah listened carefully as I outlined my case. Face to face with her, it was hard to summon the sense of outrage I had felt in my therapist's office. Sarah avoided eye contact but nodded intently as I spoke, making the strange *hmm-hmm* sound in the back of her throat that she often deployed when confronted with difficult subjects.

'I really, really think you should see somebody, you know, a professional counsellor, to talk this through,' I told her. 'Barnardos has a support group for mothers just like you. Perhaps you could give them a ring?'

'I will, I will for sure, Caitríona,' Sarah reassured me. 'I have so many issues, so many issues . . .' Her voice trailed off. 'But don't worry about me. I'll be fine, I will.'

I was not convinced that Sarah would be fine, but the conversation nonetheless felt like a breakthrough. Although I had not been able to summon the courage to tell Sarah exactly how much I was struggling under the weight of the secret, I had found the nerve to probe for more details about my birth father and to suggest that Sarah find a therapist. Discussing how we could reach each other more easily, I had also proposed that she open an email account. Sarah was non-committal – there was no computer at home, she told me – but she promised to look into it. I left the Marine Hotel feeling buoyed and empowered. For once we had addressed things head-on. I felt hopeful for the future, encouraged that Sarah would find someone to confide in, that she had begun the first steps towards revealing her secret.

Sarah's first email, sent five weeks after that meeting, was confirmation that she had listened to me. I felt elated as I clicked on the 'reply' button and began to compose my response. Perhaps, I thought to myself as I typed a warm and heartfelt message, we had begun to make a breakthrough.

I had other reasons to be happy that February morning. Just a couple of weeks earlier, Dan and I had discovered that I was pregnant with our second child. My journalism career was beginning to take off, and despite the exhaustion that the first trimester brings I was working hard, filing features every week on American life for the *Irish Independent*. Sarah's emails, meanwhile, started coming thick and fast.

I'm really loving this . . . I must have been asleep for the last twenty years.

But like most of our face-to-face conversations, our internet exchanges lacked any real substance. Sarah's emails were short, breezy and light on details. They gave no real insight into her life, her children, her thoughts or emotions. They kept me firmly at arm's length. Undeterred, I wrote long and newsy missives in return, full of anecdotes about Liam, our life in Washington, our travels to California to visit Dan's family. Occasionally I alluded to the conversation that we had had several months before, tentatively enquiring as to whether Sarah had made good on her promise to join a support group or seek professional help. But Sarah's brief responses never addressed these questions.

By the summer of 2007 I was struggling physically and emotionally with the exhausting demands of stay-at-home parenting and a freelance journalism career. As my pregnancy progressed and the demands on my time grew, I found fewer opportunities to see my therapist. The pressure valve was still rumbling. I was beginning to feel an anger towards Sarah that surprised me with its intensity. As the humidity of the Washington summer descended, Sarah's emails kept coming but I began to ignore them.

June 12 – Hope you are all in great form . . . Read your features, they were excellent as usual. If you can spare a minute let me know how things are. I love hearing from you, Lots of love, Sarah xxxxxxxxx

I didn't reply.

July 17 – Caitríona, Dan and Liam, a big hello from Dublin I hope you are all ok as I haven't heard from you lately. It could be my emails are not reaching you. I don't feel very confident on the keyboard. Saw your features . . . well done . . . I know you are very busy but if you get a minute send me a short email. Lots of love, Sarah xxxxxxx

I didn't reply.

August 13 – Caitríona, Dan and Liam, how are you? I really hope you are all ok. I haven't heard from you in a while. I have read your last three articles and really enjoyed them. Thinking of you a lot these days as your due date is so soon. I am wondering if you got my last emails or are you sick of me? I wouldn't blame you. If you have a spare minute let me know you are ok. Lots of love, Sarah xxxxxx

At last, some authenticity: '. . . are you sick of me? I wouldn't blame you.' My brain suddenly felt on fire. I wanted to rage, to scream, to pound my fists on the table. *Yes, I am sick of you. Sick of being kept a secret. Sick of you stringing me along. Sick of you treating me like shit. Sick of you denying my son.*

With just a few weeks left before my due date, I began to compose a letter. As with my first letter to her nearly eight years before, I agonized over every sentence. Still not feeling entirely certain that I was doing the right thing, I called Catherine for support. She agreed to look at a draft when it was complete. I fine-tuned the letter some more, deleting passages, struggling to strike the right tone. I sent the letter to Catherine. She responded to say that it was honest and forthright but perhaps I could find ways to 'soften it around the edges'. Her reply gave me pause. Maybe I was overreacting, going too hard on Sarah? I worried that the letter would send Sarah into an emotional spiral. Maybe this was all just the result of pregnancy hormones? Perhaps I should wait until the baby was born and then reassess?

But I had spent nearly eight years holding my tongue. It was time to speak my mind. Wanting to give Sarah advance notice, I sent her a message to say that I would soon email a letter. There was no response. I was surprised by this: Sarah had seemed so desperate to hear back from me. Was she now punishing me in return?

Three days later, with the late-afternoon sun streaming in through the French doors of our living room, I read over my letter one last time. It was now or never. I took a deep breath and placed the cursor over the 'send' key. I clicked the mouse and watched the message flash across my screen: *Message Successfully Sent.*

Dear Sarah,

Many thanks for your emails. I'm sorry it's taken me so long to reply. I can't quite explain the delay. Part of me wanted to sit down and write you a breezy note with news from Washington but another part of me couldn't bring myself to do so. Perhaps this letter will be a means of explaining.

I'm having a hard time with the nature of our relationship right now. In truth, I've been having a hard time with it for quite some time but my feelings seem to have culminated of late. Perhaps it's the imminent birth of my second child; perhaps it's just a weariness of continued secrecy after this length of time — but whatever the reason it explains my inability to contact you. I'm sorry if this has caused you any pain or worry.

Please bear with me as I struggle to explain my feelings. And I want to assure you right now that I hold no grudge or animosity or ill feelings towards you. I just want to establish as honest a dialogue as possible so we can clear this hurdle and move on into the future.

The last time we met I struggled to be as completely honest with you as I possibly could. It was one of the frankest conversations we've ever had — but it still fell short of all that I wanted to say. I left the Marine in Sutton feeling lighter than I had in many years — I had overcome my fear to ask you gently to consider some sort of counselling; I had asked you to consider another means of contact apart from our brief telephone calls; and I had asked for you to talk about my beginnings — and the relationship you had with my father.

But there was so much more that I wanted to say but — for many reasons — could not. After so many years I had hoped that this relationship would have become easier. But with the passing of time I sometimes feel as though the relationship has become something of a burden for me to carry. Your inability to reveal our secret has weighed on me in many ways and made me feel unworthy of my origins – and of myself. I wanted to tell you that I've become increasingly tired of meeting in hotel lobbies across Dublin, acting an ill-fitting role in a long-running play that I no longer feel comfortable with, or understand.

I understand – more than anyone – the great, great trauma you experienced with my conception and birth, and the loneliness and ache you must have felt in the years after my adoption. I understand too – more than anyone – how impossible it must be for you to confront this secret now and to reveal it to your dear husband and family. And I understand your fear that everything may come crashing around your ears once you do.

Having said that, Sarah, your secret has become my secret and it is a burden that is beginning to weigh very heavily for me. Since we have got to know each other I feel as though I have been very open with you. In fact, I have laid myself bare to you over the past eight years. I have opened the door to my heart and my life but I feel – very painfully – as though I have gotten very little in return. I am delighted that my family have eagerly embraced you and they have done so without judgement or bias. I was careful to include you as much as possible in my wedding, pregnancies, the birth of Liam and my travels across the globe.

But I feel as though I am still waiting for you to open yourself to me. I believe that my life is very much an open book whereas your private life is, to all intents and purposes, off limits. It was years before you showed me photographs of my siblings – something I never asked you to do but desperately wanted. I have yet to see a picture of my sister, which, I admit, is a disappointment. I tread carefully when asking questions about your family and feel grateful when you share news of their recent exploits.

In relation to my father, I am naturally quite curious and would like to be able to ask you about him. I do feel that I have the right to know the story of my beginnings and birth but increasingly I feel that the story of your relationship with my father is somehow off limits. But I'm curious about him – about that part of my DNA – and would like to be able to ask you about him without feeling as though I have no right to do so.

Sarah, I'm not necessarily asking you to reveal me to your family. In fact, amidst all the confusion of my current state of mind, I'm beginning to feel as though that is something that I don't want at this stage. I'm finding it hard to process our relationship and I don't think that right now I could handle the emotional turmoil that meeting new members might bring.

To be completely honest I'm not sure what I want. But I think mostly I want a mutually respectful relationship where I don't feel as though I'm beholden to a dark secret so shameful that we must meet incognito and discuss anything but the real reason that has brought us together.

You have been a wonderful friend to me since we met and I am forever grateful for the immense generosity that you have showered on me. And I know – very keenly – how much you love me and how desperately you want this secrecy to end.

If there is anything that I could ask it would be that you please, please, please reach out for some professional help to guide you through the emotional rollercoaster that you have endured since you gave me up all those decades ago. I have been seeing a therapist for some time now and it is a wonderful feeling to be able to talk about these complex emotions without judgement or fear.

I feel very strongly that some type of counselling or support network could help you in a very profound way. I really believe that it would help us overcome this bump in our road – for that is all that it is – and put us on a better track towards a more stable, loving and equal relationship. I would ask that you consider this proposition for my sake and for yours. I think that, considering the great burden I have carried for you since our first meeting in

*December 1999, it is a small thing to ask. (Perhaps Catherine
could help you in this regard.)*

*I want more than anything else to have you in my life. I'm sure we
can work this out.*

*With love,
Caitríona*

That night I slept fitfully. Early the following morning I
heaved my swollen belly out of bed and tiptoed to the computer to check email. There was no response. All morning
and afternoon I returned to my laptop obsessively, eliciting
concerned looks from Dan who, I later learned, was beginning to worry about the effects of this emotional rollercoaster
on our unborn child.

Finally, three days after sending the letter, I opened my
laptop and found a response.

*Caitríona, I have just read your letter and I know exactly how you are
feeling. I have had those feelings and hating myself for ages. I haven't
had the nerve to phone in a long time because it all seems so unfair to
you. I keep wondering if you had the baby but I can't pick up the phone.
I feel a total mess. Didn't see your email warning me about your letter
last week because [my brother] died suddenly that evening . . . I wasn't
totally honest with you when I said nobody knew about you. They knew
in the home place but my father couldn't accept it and didn't speak to me
for years. Please reply to this email if you can. Will text you again
tomorrow. Thinking of you a lot these days. Love, Sarah. Xxxxxxxx*

I stared blankly at the screen. Time slowed as my mind
struggled to process what I had just read. I couldn't decide
which piece of information felt more shocking: Sarah's obvious anguish, the fact that my letter had reached her in the
midst of a bereavement or the revelation that – despite

everything Sarah had ever said – her family in the 'home place' knew that she had given birth in 1972.

I thought back to that afternoon in Tuzla in August 1999 when, pen poised over paper, I had listened intently as Catherine told me what she knew of Sarah's life. That day I had written: *family doesn't know/husband doesn't know.* In our subsequent meetings, Sarah told me that not only were her husband and children ignorant of my existence but that she had hidden her pregnancy and my birth from her father and her siblings. (Her mother had died shortly before Sarah became pregnant.) Even the letter from St Patrick's Guild to my parents in July 1996 had made reference to the fact that 'to the best of our knowledge her father or members of her family were not aware of her pregnancy'.

Now, in an email, I was learning that this narrative was a lie. What did that mean? What purpose did hiding this information serve? Had Sarah been worried that I would travel back to her childhood home to confront her siblings, to reclaim my land? What else was she keeping from me?

My unborn child gave a sudden and sharp kick, jolting me back into the present. I shivered, despite the August heat, and reached for a throw to wrap round my bare shoulders. I read the email once more: 'hating myself for ages . . . I feel a total mess . . . haven't had the nerve to phone'. The shock I felt at Sarah's sudden revelation now gave way to an enormous wave of guilt over having sent the letter at such a disastrous time. I imagined Sarah, already grief-stricken over the loss of a sibling, opening my email, unaware of the ticking bomb inside. I felt like a louse: neurotic, needy, the worst child in the world. The rage that had built over days and weeks and years receded once more. I should never have spoken my mind, I thought to myself, I should have left things alone.

*

The birth of my daughter Caoimhe in early September 2007 helped temper the awkwardness that had settled between Sarah and me. By the close of that year we were back in regular contact and I was once again emailing her newsy updates about her latest grandchild. But the issues I had raised in my letter were never discussed.

Early in the new year, unable to attend regular therapy owing to the demands of two small children, I signed up for an adoptee support group that met one evening a month. While Dan put the kids to bed, I took a metro out to an adoption agency in Bethesda where I sat in a circle and ate pizza and drank Diet Coke with other adult adoptees. But I found the dynamics of group therapy unsettling. I hung back shyly in the circle, happy to listen but too reticent to share. I felt as though I had little in common with these American adoptees, the majority of whom had been adopted internationally and had grown up knowing who their birth parents were. Sarah's secret and the nature of our relationship fell outside the prevailing narrative of this group. My story felt prehistoric, an anomaly, a relic of Ireland's dreary past. The others in the group struggled to understand my story while I began to resent theirs. Eventually I stopped going.

That same spring, I left the kids at home with Dan one Saturday afternoon and drove to a university campus in the suburbs to attend a conference on adoption. At a panel discussion on reunion, I sat and listened as a young man made an emotional presentation about his recent search for his birth mother. There on the podium, flanking him on either side, sat his birth mother and his adoptive mother. The birth mother spoke tearfully about her delight in having been located. Following their reunion, this mother threw her twenty-five-year-old son a retroactive baby shower, inviting friends and family who hadn't known about his existence.

She laughed as she told the audience how she decorated her house in blue ribbons and balloons and put a giant blue cardboard stork on the front door.

The baby shower anecdote struck me as creepy, not to mention disrespectful towards the young man's adoptive mother. This birth mother was, it seemed to me, coming on too strong, and I wondered whether the ménage could continue along this manic trajectory. At the same time, watching this happy trio hold hands, I fought the urge to cry. I thought of Sarah, back in Ireland, skulking through her double life. I thought of myself, sitting resentfully in a soulless conference centre on a weekend afternoon, still trying, after all these years, to make sense of our relationship.

IO

On a rainy, cold afternoon in March 2009 I take four-year-old Liam for his annual check-up at the dentist. We are late to the appointment and a surly receptionist at the front desk is unimpressed by my apologies. Sitting on my right hip, wide-eyed and cheery, is eighteen-month-old Caoimhe. With beautiful almond-shaped eyes and a dark thatch of hair that shoots straight up from the centre of her head, Caoimhe is a child who elicits smiles of delight from passers-by. But right now, in this darkened waiting room, even Caoimhe's cherubic charm is powerless in raising the spirits of the churlish receptionist.

Minutes later Liam is lying flat on his back, dwarfed by the adult proportions of the dental chair. Unusually uncooperative, he whimpers and squirms as a weary-looking hygienist tries to coax him into opening his mouth. Bouncing Caoimhe up and down on my hip, I try to distract Liam with songs and tricks. Nothing works. Finally, in desperation, I turn to my last resort: bribery. Liam's mouth snaps wide open the instant he hears promise of a small *Star Wars* toy – his obsession of the moment – in return for his immediate cooperation.

Half an hour later I am lugging our double stroller down the steps of a large bookshop. Liam scampers ahead to the children's section, where the *Star Wars* toys await, while I follow close behind. As I unbuckle Caoimhe from the stroller, my mobile phone rings. I look down at the screen to see an unfamiliar number. I pick up to hear a woman's voice.

'Hello, is that Caitríona?'

'Hi, yes, this is Caitríona.'

'Oh, hello,' the woman says. 'This is Josephine.'

Josephine. My mind struggles to connect the voice to the name. I have no idea who this is. I pause, furrowing my brow as I look down at Caoimhe, whose spiky head is now buried in a brightly coloured baby book.

'Josephine?' I say, trying not to appear rude.

'Do you remember?' the woman says. 'We've been in email touch about my website.'

I snap to attention, immediately understanding. Scanning the bookstore, I search for a quiet corner where I can talk in private while also keeping an eye on the kids. My heart is racing. This is a potentially life-altering phone call and I'm not sure where to begin.

A couple of years earlier, frustrated by Sarah's evasiveness on the subject, I had begun to hunt online for my biological father. I knew a few things about him: his name (here I'll call him Tom), the village where he came from, the fact that he was working as a builder at the time of his liaison with Sarah, and that he had another girlfriend at the same time, who he'd gone on to marry (I'll call her Aileen). Sitting at my desk during the day – often on a pressing deadline for my paper in Dublin – I found my mind wandering, my fingers typing various combinations of these scanty details into a search engine.

Eventually, my internet sleuthing identified two possible candidates. One was a midlands farmer whose home and farm improvements had given rise to planning permission notices. The name and county of origin fitted but the profession was off. The other candidate – a man on the opposite side of the country – fitted the profile but he was much too young. Perhaps he was a son? Or a nephew?

The internet searches felt illicit and wrong, not least because I had told Sarah that I had no interest in contacting Tom. But by that stage I had reached a dead end in my relationship with Sarah, and I needed more. I didn't tell Sarah or anyone else about my online stalking, not even Dan. The pursuit seemed gratuitous, greedy, and I worried about being judged. I knew that I was becoming an adoption bore, obsessed with uncovering my identity. But each time I opened my laptop I found myself returning to the search.

One night in late January 2009, after the kids had gone to bed, I sat down at our dining-room table to begin an assignment for my paper. Dan sat across from me, reading. Exhausted from a day at home with the kids and daunted by the prospect of writing a 1,200-word feature, I began to procrastinate, searching again for my father's name. This time there was a new hit: a website exploring the genealogy of a woman's family in the west of Ireland. One of the surnames in the extended family matched Tom's. My heartbeat quickened as I scrolled through the pages: the site was largely devoted to the tiny village where Tom had been born.

'Take a look at this,' I said as I swivelled my laptop round to face Dan. 'I think I've just found my father.'

Over the course of the following days I returned again and again to the website. It appeared to be maintained by two amateur genealogists, one of whom was called Josephine. If my theory was correct, Josephine was probably my cousin. I considered my options. I could ignore the information and just get on with my life. Or I could approach Josephine and try, through her, to establish contact with Tom. The latter option seemed dangerous, bordering on an invasion of my birth father's privacy. Most adoption experts advised against searching for a birth parent without the assistance of a social worker. But I told myself that my snooping was just an exercise to confirm that Tom was alive. I had no intention of showing up on his doorstep to cause a scene.

The journalist in me knew that it would be negligent not to cross-reference the information that I had on Tom before contacting Josephine. But that option meant having to go back to the one person in my life who knew the truth – Sarah. For nearly a decade I had spun the lie that I would never search for Tom, that he served no purpose in my life. I was worried that if I told her about this quest it would send her into a tailspin. Perhaps she would interpret my interest in Tom as a rejection of her, of the two of us? And so in early February, while composing an email to Sarah, I decided to lie.

I've been thinking about us and about my beginnings and trying to make sense of it all. And – as bizarre as it all seems – I want to double-check the name of my father. Was it Tom _____ from _____? I'm sorry to ask but I'm trying to build a narrative and for some reason this is important. Would you be comfortable writing me an email explaining my beginnings? How you met him? What the story was? I don't mean for this to be an intrusion but I feel as though I need to know this story. It might make my overall picture seem complete.

The deference of that email now astonishes me. I am tiptoeing around my past, afraid to plumb Sarah for details. I have allowed Sarah to become keeper of our story, to hold it, like a stack of secret cards, close to her chest. I have also – just like her – become adept at lying. But part of me didn't care. For over three decades Sarah had kept me a secret. Now I had a secret of my own.

Days passed without a reply. Finally, nearly two weeks after sending the email to Sarah, my patience ran out. On 17 February I began to compose an email to Josephine.

Sarah had long ago told me that Tom had a sidekick in the town where they dated – a younger brother who accompanied him on his nightly forays into the pubs. I decided to use this man's name alongside Tom's in my first email to Josephine, hoping it would somehow help conceal my purpose. Trying to give the impression – without directly saying so – that I was some distant American cousin with a penchant for genealogy, I began to type.

Dear Josephine,

My name is Caitríona and I am writing to you from Washington, DC. I came across your wonderful site while googling the _____ family name in County _____. I'm interested in tracing some current members of the _____ family who may still be living in the area. Their names are Tom and _____ _____, born circa 19__, and I believe they once – or still do – work in the construction industry. Any help you could give me in tracing these family members would be most appreciated. Thanks so much and the best of luck with your wonderful site.

Nine days later there was a reply.

Hi Caitríona,

Thank you for your email and I am sorry for the delay in responding. I do have a first cousin, Tom _____ from _____, who would fit your description, however, his last name is not an uncommon name in County _____, and I do not have his current contact details. If you can tell me more about the persons you are seeking and the reason, and if it seems to be the right Tom, I can try to get your contact details and message to him via his brother.

Best wishes,
Josephine

Josephine's reply was friendly but she was rightly sceptical of this stranger seeking information out of the blue. The ball was now back in my court. How should I respond?

My thoughts turned to a dinner party in Washington that I had attended a couple of months before. That night I had sat next to a Frenchwoman, Charlotte, the wife of an old acquaintance of Dan's. Charlotte, a young mother, ran a freelance private investigation firm out of her home in Washington. I spent most of that night grilling her about her work, fascinated by the stories that she spun. Over dessert I filled her in on the saga of my affair with Sarah. Sympathetic and intrigued, she told me about colleagues who specialized in reuniting adopted children with their birth parents. Now, contemplating my next move in this chess game with Josephine, I thought about Charlotte. Lost relatives and secret affairs were her bread and butter and I figured she'd know what to do. I typed her a quick email telling her of the latest development in my quest. What, I asked, would you do if you were me?

Charlotte replied the next day:

From what I was told by private investigators specializing in adoption searches, phone or in-person contacts are the best but it's more difficult from here: you can tell this cousin – if she can forward your request to his brother – that an old friend is trying to make contact, mention your mom's name as you said, maybe another detail that could spark his interest, and that you'd rather talk to him personally. Leave your name and phone number or email address to that effect so that he can call you. If your birth father knows that there was a pregnancy, he may suspect something and may give it a try. If he has no idea that there was a pregnancy, you'll probably need to confide in the brother. Most people react nicely if they can see that you're honest and that you're asking for their help because you don't want to barge in on his

149

*family and disrupt things. From what I understand, it's important to
say pretty early on that they had a child born in XX year, that you are
this child and that you're doing OK, got well taken care of and just
wanted a chance to contact him. Also, by now, his other kids, if he has
other kids, must be grown up so it shouldn't be as difficult as if he was
still raising young children. And you never know, sometimes birth
fathers keep the contact info for a while and call or email later, after
thinking about it, after divorcing the current wife they're afraid of . . .*

Charlotte's advice seemed very solid. I composed an email
to Josephine:

Dear Josephine,

*Many thanks for your note. And this time it's my turn to apologize
for the delay in responding . . . I'm an old friend of Tom's who would
like to get in touch with him. If you could let him know, via his
brother, that I'm related to Sarah Smith who he knew from _____
in 1971. I would love to chat to him privately, if he had the time . . .*

I hit 'send' and watched the message evaporate off the
screen. I took a deep breath and placed my hands across my
stomach, aware of the first pinpricks of anxiety beginning to
spread. Unsatisfied, I clicked on the 'sent mail' folder, reread
the email and immediately had second thoughts. What if
Josephine called Tom or his brother out of the blue? I felt
out of control, a danger to myself. I should be escorted away
from my laptop, I thought, before I did more damage. I
picked up the phone to call Dan at work but got voicemail.
Desperate to reach Dan, I forwarded him the email I had just
sent Josephine with an additional message:

*What do you think? Have I lost it completely? Wrote this on the
advice of Charlotte. Couldn't help myself.*

Some minutes later Dan replied:

No, you haven't lost it at all. I think you handled it perfectly.

Four days later, another reply from Josephine: she would try to contact her cousins 'in the next few days'.

I began to panic. This was moving much too quickly. I imagined Josephine calling Tom's brother: 'Hey, there's this Irishwoman over in America who says that she knows you and Tom. Something to do with another woman that you both knew back in the early 1970s, someone called Sarah Smith?' I imagined Tom's brother taking down the details. I imagined him a few days later sitting in Tom's living room, across from my birth father and his wife, Aileen, recounting the bizarre phone call that he'd had from their long-lost cousin Josephine. I imagined Sarah's name detonating like a landmine in the middle of Tom's living room.

I needed to slow things down. I hit 'compose mail' in my email account and began to type furiously. I thought about what Charlotte had advised the previous week: *Most people react nicely if they can see that you're honest and that you're asking for their help.* After a couple of pleasantries, I got straight to the point.

> *I apologize for bothering you with all this. If it is at all possible, I would be so grateful if you could get in touch with Tom or his brother privately (preferably Tom, if at all possible) to convey my desire to get in touch. The matter is a little sensitive. I'm sorry to be so cryptic. If you'd be more comfortable speaking to me in person about this please don't hesitate to call me anytime . . .*

Three days later, on that rainy Tuesday afternoon at the bookstore, Josephine called. Her voice was warm and friendly, and I immediately felt at ease.

'So,' she said, after we had exchanged some small talk. 'What's all this about?'

I paused, not knowing where to begin. I racked my brain for a way to talk about Tom without outing him as my father. Babbling incoherently, I told Josephine about my internet sleuthing and the surprise I felt on the night that I stumbled across her website.

The silence on the other end of the phone told me I was not making any sense. It was time to come clean.

'Well, the fact of the matter is – I'm not quite sure how to say this – but I think that Tom might actually be my father.'

There was a pause on the line as Josephine absorbed the news.

'Ah,' she said softly, as I held my breath waiting for her response. 'I figured you were going to say something like that.'

Josephine was kind but understandably cautious. While keeping an eye on Liam and Caoimhe, I told her in hushed tones about my search for Sarah, our eight-year relationship and how I had only recently started looking for my birth father. Josephine, non-committal, asked for some time to think about my request that she contact Tom on my behalf. We agreed that we would chat again over the coming days.

That night I sat down and wrote Josephine another email to thank her for her kindness. I included some photographs of the kids and one of myself.

It was so lovely to talk with you and share my tale. I fully understand if you feel at any point that this quest is too complicated or difficult to pursue. Or if you feel that it might cause anguish or heartache to Tom or his family. My need at this stage is just to let him know of my existence, to give him an update of my life thus far, and to wish him well. My reunion with my birth mother has taught me not to have any great expectations in the search for my biological parents.

Three days later there was a cheerful response.

Hi Caitríona,

Sorry for the delay in getting back to you and thank you so much for the email and the pictures – what a handsome bunch you all are. You have to be related . . . I have thought over what we talked about a lot and I have decided that I will broach the subject with Tom. I have tried to telephone him a couple of times but have never been able to get him at home again. I will try again . . . probably a bit later in the week. I too enjoyed our chat and I hope that we can talk again soon.

Love and best wishes,
Josephine

I was moved by Josephine's kindness. Her willingness to contact Tom was more than I could reasonably have hoped for. Worn down by eight years of secrecy, I was accustomed to being kept in the dark. Now, a stranger who barely knew me was offering to lift me up into the light.

Three days later Josephine emailed again to say she had called Tom's home and left a message with his eldest son. Tom had three grown children, Josephine told me, two boys and a girl. I forwarded Josephine's email to Dan with the subject line 'more siblings!' I was experiencing the rush that comes with every biological echo. Three new half-siblings. Add this to Sarah's total and that made six. I was giddy with excitement.

And then, out of the blue, an email from Sarah, a response to my email sent weeks earlier to cross-check information on Tom. It was obvious that Sarah was rattled by my request.

*I promise I will write you a letter with all that information. I am not
very good at emailing. You are the only one I email. I hope you are
still at the same address. I promise I will write to you at the weekend.
I can't bear to think of all the pain I am causing you. Lots and lots
of love to you all.*

Sarah xxxxxx

Five days later I open my inbox and find two emails from
Sarah. I read the first:

*. . . Thank you so much for your kind email. I have decided to email
you instead of writing. I met Tom _____ in 1970 when I settled
in _____ and taught in a little country school. I fell head over
heels for him. He was so handsome. I was really smitten. He worked
on the buildings in _____ with his brother _____ and lived in
_____ at the time. As I said I was madly in love with him but he
was in love with Aileen from _____ and they married*

The first email breaks off there. I open the second.

*Caitríona . . . I got really agitated and started pressing all the wrong
keys. I was afraid I would lose the email so I decided to send it
quickly.*

The second email supplies a few more details – the names
of Tom's sisters, and the city where Aileen, Tom's other girlfriend, worked during the week. The information dovetails
perfectly with the things I have learned from Josephine: it is
clear that I have the right man.

A few days later Josephine calls to say that she has reached
Tom on his mobile phone. I can tell by the tone of her voice
that the news isn't good.

'He was in his car,' she tells me. 'The line wasn't very good.

He had to pull over so we could talk. I gave him all of the details. He was having a hard time remembering so far back. The name of your birth mother didn't ring a bell but he said he'd think about it. I'm to call him again in another couple of days.'

I am incredulous. Flat-out denial I had expected. Anger, rage. But an evasive, head-scratching 'I can't quite recall' is hard to credit.

'Did he say anything else?' I ask.

'Not very much. It was a very short call. He basically said, "Sure that was a long time ago. I wouldn't be remembering that."'

Sure that was a long time ago. I wouldn't be remembering that. In a way it fits the image of the man sitting in the pub thirty-seven years earlier, regarding his pint, pretending not to hear the news that he is to become a father. First deafness, now amnesia.

I sit and write a letter to Tom. My hope is that Josephine will be able to give it to him – or at least read it to him over the phone the next time they speak.

I begin by explaining who I am and who my birth mother is, and I describe how my work in Bosnia prompted me to establish contact with Sarah.

I never anticipated trying to find you but my feelings have changed considerably over the years. I am unable to explain my change of heart. I simply – like the families I worked so closely with in Bosnia – need to know the truth. I need to know where I came from, who my parents are, what type of people they are and whether we share any similarities – good or bad.

I know that Josephine's telephone call will have come as a great shock to you and I apologize sincerely for contacting you out of the blue . . .

155

I am writing to you from Washington, DC, where I have been living and working for the last four years as a journalist for the Irish Independent. The greatest news that I can share is that I am the mother of two deliciously delightful children, Liam (4) and Caoimhe (18 months). They are the light of my life and the product of my extremely happy marriage to an amazing man, Dan De Luce, who I fell madly in love with in Bosnia ten years ago. Dan and I have lived in many places together – Bosnia, Holland, London, Iran and, now, America. We have been very fortunate in our adventures together, the friends that we've made, and the life we now lead.

I have been very fortunate too in my wonderful parents and family who adopted me following my birth in Holles Street hospital on the 19th April 1972. I spent six weeks in a baby home in Dublin before my parents drove me home to begin my new life with my older brother and sister in a modest suburb in north Dublin.

My parents raised me to work hard, to be kind and respectful to others and to enjoy all that life has to offer. Our family wasn't perfect by any means but I was loved fiercely by my parents, who have always considered me their own. I remain forever grateful to them and for all that they've done for me.

I don't want to cause any trouble in your life or any pain to your family. I merely wanted to reach out and to let you know of my existence. I would very much like to speak to you and perhaps, one day, meet in person. That would mean the world to me.

I wish you nothing but great happiness.

With love,
Caitríona

I wait. I go about my ordinary life. I care for my children, I write frivolous features for my newspaper, I cook dinner for friends at the weekend, I make love to Dan. Things are at once impossibly normal and immensely fragile. I feel as though I might, at a moment's notice, shatter into a million

pieces. I curse the two people who gave me life, one determined to keep me at arm's length, the other unwilling to
admit he knows anything about me.

The call comes a few days later. Tom has had time to think,
Josephine tells me, but he really can't remember so far back.
He doesn't want to see the letter. 'Caitríona, I am so very
sorry.' I can hear the sorrow and frustration in her voice.

'There's nothing that you can do,' I tell her. 'I'm just so
incredibly grateful for all that you've done so far. Really, I
can't thank you enough.'

'Perhaps he'll come around in time,' she says.

'Perhaps,' I say, already knowing that he is lost for ever.

'I did tell him,' Josephine says, 'and I hope you don't mind
my doing so, that you are a daughter that any father would be
proud of.'

I feel a lump rising in my throat.

'I mean that, Caitríona. A daughter to be very proud of.'

11

In February 2011, now actively researching this book, I travelled on my own to Ireland to interview Liam, Mary and Thérèse and to poke around the Archdiocese's archives. On that short visit I met Sarah three times at the Marine Hotel in Sutton. Though less salubrious than the Westbury, the Marine was spacious and relaxed and featured a large garden with low-slung trees that I had loved to climb as a child. For about seven years it had been our main haunt.

That day, in a corner of the bar, hidden from view, I turned on my tape recorder and asked Sarah to tell me the story of her romance with Tom. Sarah knew of my tentative plan to write a book and had encouraged the project. Courageously, she had given me permission to use her story on the condition that I protect not just her identity, but those of Tom and their respective families. I remember sitting down with Sarah, directing her to the seat right next to mine, thinking she might speak more freely if we were not making eye contact.

It is difficult now, many years on, to listen to the tape of that conversation. Sarah's voice seems so small and heartsick, so full of pain. With hindsight, I feel bad about putting her through such an interrogation. But I was being driven by a force stronger than my need to please Sarah. It was imperative that Sarah share the story, *our story*. It was only right that I understood how it had all began.

The account that follows is based on that interview with Sarah in February 2011, on subsequent conversations and correspondence with her, and on interviews I later conducted with people who lived in the town where she and Tom conducted their relationship.

In the summer of 1970, Sarah packed a large suitcase and climbed aboard a bus that would take her to a sleepy town in the midlands of the country. She was on her way to her first job, a trainee-teacher position in a small country school. With a teacher-training degree under her belt, she had been dispatched to this little town in a part of Ireland that she knew nothing about. It was sink-or-swim time. If she could impress the head teacher and not make any major mistakes, then she'd be in line for a permanent job.

Sarah spent the first week of her new life staying at a bed-and-breakfast on the main street of the town. In the teachers' lounge one day she heard about a boarding house on the edge of town run by a friendly couple called O'Connor who had trained in the hospitality business in a prestigious hotel in Dublin and who now offered room and full board at a reasonable rate for young professionals like herself. By week's end she had moved into a shared room with another female lodger on the second floor of the O'Connor home. The room was small with two narrow single beds, a large built-in wardrobe and a hand basin with shelving and a mirror.

There were thirteen other lodgers staying at the O'Connors': teachers, bankers and the odd Garda. At 1 p.m. sharp, Monday to Friday, everyone would leave their respective workplaces to return to the house for Mrs O'Connor's delicious home-cooked lunches: homemade soup followed by a big meaty main course – roast beef, roast stuffed chicken, corned beef, braised beef stew, shepherd's pie. Sarah ensured that she left room for Mrs O'Connor's famed desserts: apple and lemon meringue pie, trifle, rice pudding, highland tart, sponge flan and steamed pudding served with lashings of hot custard or cream.

At 6 p.m. the lodgers would convene again for 'tea': meat salad, stuffed beef tomatoes, fish cakes, lamb chops or a mixed grill. Mrs O'Connor's young daughters ferried in pots of tea and thick slices of fruitcake or plates of hot buttered scones. Sometimes after tea the lodgers would gather in the living room to chat and gossip, play a round of cards or listen politely as a fellow boarder inexpertly banged out a couple of show tunes on the piano in the corner. Later they might leave the house in huddles of twos and threes for the pub across the street. The place to be seen was in the 'singing lounge', a smoky bar with a clearing in the corner where a small band of local musicians would belt out the hits of the day. By closing time, patrons would be clamouring to take over the microphone, their vocal cords loosened by one too many pints.

Down the street from where Sarah lodged, a local hall held dances on Saturday nights, the snooker and ping-pong tables put away to make room for the mass of shuffling bodies. Once a year, a big personality like Bridie Gallagher, the 'Girl from Donegal', would come to town, causing a rush on tickets that would sell out in hours. Other times, popular show bands like Joe Dolan and the Drifters would play in a dance hall a few towns over, prompting a queue to form early on a Saturday evening at the local bus terminal.

Sometimes on a Sunday afternoon Sarah would meet a friend at the local cinema for a matinee double bill, slipping out at the intermission to rush to the shop across the street and stock up on sweets and ice cream for the second film. Courting couples mostly sat upstairs in 'the gods', while the front row offered the cheapest viewing at just eight pennies a seat. Sarah and her friends sat in the middle, paying a shilling apiece.

Navigating the beeswax-polish-scented halls of the local school that first term, Sarah diligently applied herself to her new job, becoming familiar with the rhythms of the class-room, exercising tentative authority over her young charges and earning the respect of the head, who glided in and out of her classroom on constant, reproachful alert. By Christmas 1970 Sarah felt sure-footed and secure in her new life, happy and at ease as she packed her suitcase to head home to her family for the two-week Christmas break.

I like to imagine Sarah in these early days, full of hope and excitement, an independent young woman on the cusp of bright beginnings, unaware of the wave that was about to break over her life and sweep her away. I see her making her tentative way in the world, tall and beautiful, captivating in her own quiet way, oblivious of the effect that she had on men. I want to shout out to this young woman to take care and to watch out.

It was at a house party after a night in a local pub that Sarah first locked eyes with the man who would become my bio-logical father.

A jaunty, charismatic lad about town, Tom worked as a builder, putting up new housing estates around the area. At night, he was part of a group of boisterous young men who drove souped-up cars. One glance in his direction and Sarah was smitten.

Unbeknownst to Sarah, Tom was already 'doing a line' with someone else. Aileen was a catch: a pretty girl from a prominent local family. But that month Tom and Aileen had broken up and Tom's eyes were wandering. They fell upon Sarah: tall, lean and beautiful with high cheekbones and wide expressive eyes. By evening's end they had arranged to meet again later in the week with the promise that Tom would take

Sarah out for a spin in his silver sports car. 'It was a bit of a banger,' Sarah told me, 'but I didn't care. After meeting him that first night I felt as high as a kite.'

Soon they were an unofficial item. Very unofficial: Tom reignited his romance with Aileen, and it was clear that this relationship, given Aileen's status in the town, was one that he wanted to protect. But who said that he couldn't have a little fun on the side? Sarah was too love-struck to complain. During the week, while Aileen worked in Dublin, Sarah was Tom's girl. In the evenings she kept watch for his car on the main street, ducking into the same bar if he was there. They would chat, have a drink and leave together. 'There was no friendship. It was all very furtive. He was charming,' Sarah told me. 'I feel as though I should have said no in the beginning but I suppose I was hoping that I would be the one. Looking back, I was totally out of my depth, totally out of my depth. [Aileen] was the sophisticated one.'

'Do you remember the first time you ever saw him?'

'I do. I remember it clearly,' Sarah says. 'A group of us went out after the pub. We went out to some house, to a house party. I saw him there. I remember being very excited and fancying him. It was all off with Aileen at the time. And he was sort of into me. But there was a coolness about him. I would see him on and off during the week if I happened to be there . . . you know the way. He would never make a date and say, "I'll see you on such a day." Most of the time I just happened to be where he was and I would end up leaving with him.'

Sarah pauses. Her hand flicks to her forehead, where she absent-mindedly brushes away her hair. Her anguish is palpable. She runs her fingers along the rim of her gin and tonic and continues. 'His group of mates were this good-looking bunch. They were the big gang around town.'

She trails off. 'I just feel weird talking about this.'

My immediate instinct is to turn off the tape, to tell her that I'm sorry, that we'll chat about it another day. But instead, with a force of will that takes me by surprise, I say nothing, hoping she will continue. Sarah takes another sip of her drink.

'I feel as though I was the one who did all the running. I feel that I should have had my eyes wide open, that I was just . . . that I was mostly to blame. And I felt that just because he noticed me that I was this . . .' She pauses, searching for the right word and not coming up with it. 'But really Aileen was "the one" all of the time. I was the one sneaking in, sneaking around, even though I knew I just didn't feel comfortable with him . . . it's just that it's more exciting, in a way, with someone when you don't know where you stand.' She pauses again. 'I'm not explaining myself.'

'Don't be so hard on yourself,' I tell her gently. 'You were very young. And besides, he was going out with someone else. You can't be putting the blame entirely on yourself.'

Sarah looks up. She seems momentarily startled, as though she has just woken from a dream. She points at me, smiling. 'But that's the good ending,' she says, laying her hand gently on my arm. '*You're* the good ending. I was thinking that this morning, wondering perhaps whether all of this was meant to be.'

I smile at her, nodding.

Her smile quickly fades. She looks down at her drink. 'Only then I wondered whether you had suffered?'

'I haven't suffered, Sarah,' I tell her emphatically. 'I've had an amazing life. I'm very happy.'

'But, Caitríona, you *have* suffered. You have suffered an awful lot.' She taps her hair lightly. 'In my head, something happened after you were born. You continue on but you're not right. It's like a light going out in your head or something. But you don't end up screaming or shouting. You're just ... your head is just never the same again. You go through the motions. It's so weird. It's just so bottled up.'

She continues: 'I think it was the situation back in my childhood home that caused it. Nowadays, if you went home and said you were pregnant, that would set the ball rolling and you'd probably be given a cup of tea and told not to worry. Whereas then, it was just ...' Sarah pauses. 'It was just the end of the world.'

I never had the courage to ask Sarah that day, with the tape recorder still running, to share with me the details of her sex life with Tom. I was burning to know the specifics, the site of my conception, but the child in me was too embarrassed to ask. I decided, instead, to play detective with the facts that I had. Sarah had already told me that Tom – who, like Sarah had come to the midlands from elsewhere in Ireland in search of work – lived with a bunch of guys on the opposite side of town. 'He never invited me back there,' she told me that afternoon. 'I never saw where he lived.' I knew too that the O'Connor boarding house had a reputation as a chaste and proper establishment with zero tolerance for nocturnal visitors. That left Tom's silver banger. I suspect that this is where I was conceived sometime in the waning weeks of July 1971, the car parked beneath the leafy canopy of a country lane, the radio playing some hit song, the windows misty.

It's strange, even now, to think of Tom and Sarah as a unit, as *my parents*. I have always thought of them as two separate beings who merged momentarily to make a catastrophic mistake before drifting apart. Sarah has told me many times that she loved Tom and fervently hoped he was 'the one'. I believe, as naive as her love for him was, that had he proposed she would have married him on the spot. He, I am sure, found her beautiful and alluring, and was pleased with her willingness to play second fiddle to the sophisticated Aileen. It all seems eerily familiar: Tom dictating the terms of the affair with Sarah, just as Sarah would later do with me.

One night in October 1971, at a pub just down the street from the O'Connor boarding house, Sarah took a deep breath, plucked up her courage and blurted out to Tom that she was pregnant. For weeks she had been in denial, aware that her period was late but too paralysed by fear to accept reality. Throughout the first weeks of the new school term Sarah had struggled through each day in a cloud of anxiety and dread.

'Pregnancy is a funny thing because you don't believe you are pregnant,' Sarah told me that day in the Marine Hotel. 'You don't believe that you are [pregnant] for months and months. You are in denial. It's like those stories where you can go for nine months without even knowing. I just kept hoping that I would just get up one morning and everything would disappear. That everything would right itself.'

Taking the view that she alone had brought this calamity upon herself, Sarah felt sheepish about breaking the news to Tom. In her twisted logic, Tom's commitment to Aileen absolved him of any role in the mess that she now found herself in. She had knowingly gone along with the relationship, behind another woman's back.

'I wasn't forceful,' she told me, 'because I knew I was in the wrong. I didn't push it because I knew that I had . . . you know . . . that I shouldn't have been where I was.'

'How did he take it?' She had told me about this moment before, but I didn't want to assume I knew the full story.

'He just pretended he didn't hear. I think I left after that.

At that stage I knew I had totally lost. There was nothing, there was nothing there.'

What sort of man feigns deafness when his girlfriend sits down and tells him that she's pregnant with his child? I have replayed this scene countless times in my mind but still cannot get my head round the cruelty of that moment. I see Tom sitting there, his legs splayed, his pint sitting on the table in front of him. Suddenly, in the tumble of words coming from Sarah's mouth, he hears the word 'pregnant'. I see him silent and thoughtful, his mind racing as he tries to compute what Sarah has just said. The moment demands courage, empathy and resolve, but instead he says nothing. He reaches over and picks up his pint, a slight tremor visible in his hand as he raises the glass to his lips. Defeated by his silence, Sarah gathers up her jacket and heads for the door. It is the last time she will ever lay eyes on him.

'I wanted to go home then,' Sarah said of that moment when she stepped out on to the pavement and realized that she was on her own. 'I wanted to go home but that wasn't an option.'

At that time Sarah's family was in crisis. Several months earlier, on a sunny spring day, Sarah's mother had died of a sudden and catastrophic heart attack. The tragedy had brought chaos to the house. Sarah's father, now a widower with multiple children, had taken to his bed. There was no way Sarah could come home now and say that she was pregnant.

'My mother has just died at this point . . . Things at home were crazy, crazy, crazy,' Sarah said. 'I wanted to go home . . . [Instead] I went to a doctor and was told about a charity in Dublin. I have sort of blocked it out. It's genuine when I say that. I have blocked that time out.' At the National Maternity Hospital, in Holles Street, she was given a certificate saying that she had a kidney infection. 'I handed that in to my school and they believed it.'

I asked Sarah whether she ever contemplated – like so many other women – taking the boat across the Irish Sea for an abortion. Sarah looked horrified.

'No. No. I wouldn't even have known. No. No. No. No. As I said, I was totally gullible. I wouldn't have anyway because I couldn't kill a fly. God, no way.'

'What about the option of keeping me?' I asked. 'Did that ever cross your mind?'

'It did, but . . .' Sarah trailed off. 'I felt, you know, I left my name and address and all. I felt OK. That you'd have a good life. I knew . . . I sensed that I was there. That I was . . .' She didn't finish the sentence.

I remained silent.

'The whole thing was . . .' Sarah hesitated, searching for the right word. 'I felt I was doing the right thing.'

Sarah went home for Christmas, as usual, but did not tell anyone in her family about her pregnancy. At the end of the holidays, she packed her bags and told them she was returning to her job at the school. Instead she headed for Dublin, where the Catholic charity had secured her temporary lodgings, a house in a Dublin suburb owned by a young couple with small children. In complete anonymity and with free room and board, Sarah was guaranteed that she could stay there until her child was born. The only thing asked of her was that she occasionally help out with the family's kids. With extraordinary speed and efficiency the Irish Church and medical establishment had colluded to conceal Sarah's shameful fall.

Sarah lived quietly in her new lodgings, rarely venturing outside, her blossoming waistline visible only to Anne and

Paddy and their three young children. While Paddy was out at work, Sarah sometimes helped Anne with a little light housework, and she babysat the three kids. When Sarah had an appointment at the maternity hospital, Anne would drive her there, waiting outside until Sarah was done. The mood in the house was friendly and upbeat, and Sarah at times felt happy. But every morning when she woke, she felt a concrete block of anxiety resting on her sternum.

Sarah's recollection of her interactions with institutions during her pregnancy is a bit fuzzy, and it's not clear at what point she came into contact with St Patrick's Guild or on precisely what terms. What is clear is that, having accumulated some savings from her work as a teacher, she was able to cover the fees charged by the Guild, and thus avoid the fate of many unmarried mothers: a period of indentured servitude in a mother-and-baby home or a Magdalen Laundry.

In the early hours of 19 April 1972, Sarah felt the first pangs of labour pain. She suffered in silence for some time before quietly slipping out of bed and knocking softly on the door to the bedroom of the couple she was lodging with, asking to be driven to Holles Street. I was born at around two o'clock in the afternoon, a long-limbed baby with a mop of black hair. According to the letter sent by St Patrick's Guild to my parents in July 1996, based on a consultation of the Guild's files, Sarah's labour was 'normal', the duration '9 hours and 50 minutes', and my birth weight '3320 grams', seven pounds and five ounces.

I asked Sarah about the labour that day in February 2011, in the Marine Hotel.

'Everything went very smoothly,' she told me. 'It was easy, very easy . . . I couldn't believe it when everything was over. I thought it hadn't even started. I couldn't say that about the subsequent births. Really, it was so different. But maybe you get little graces, you know?'

Little graces. The grace of a pain-free birth in anticipation of the real agony that was to come.

'They didn't give you to me straight away,' Sarah said. 'No, they didn't. I'm sure they were aware that, you know . . .' She trailed off, unable to finish the sentence.

Back on the ward following my birth, Sarah marvelled at my long arms and legs and delighted in my lazy yawns. I was placed in a steel cot next to her bed while someone was dispatched to call St Patrick's Guild to tell them that a baby had arrived. Around her, in happy clusters, sat the adoring families of other young mothers. Babies were passed around, cooed over. Alone in her bed, without her family or her baby, Sarah watched it all.

'The nurses were very, very nice. You couldn't fault them,' Sarah recalled. 'I didn't discuss anything with the other patients but I felt as if they knew.'

'Did anyone come to visit you from St Patrick's Guild?' I asked.

'I can't remember, but I'm sure arrangements were being made behind the scenes. But I couldn't swear to that either. It's funny how you block out stuff. It's very hard to get it back.'

Sarah looked at me with a sudden realization. 'You're the very first person to ever ask me these questions,' she said.

It took a while for the significance of that statement to register: in nearly forty years this was the first time that Sarah had spoken aloud of these events. I knew I had to ask her to describe the moment when she saw me for the very last time, but I was dreading it. My heart was racing when finally I asked: 'Do you remember what it was like to leave me?'

Sarah was silent. She looked down at her hands. *I'm so sorry to ask you that*, I said to her in my mind, *I'm so, so sorry.*

'Yeah,' Sarah whispers. 'Yeah, I do.'

Her voice was tiny. 'The family that I had stayed with, they would have . . . they would have taken me back for a night or two. They came to get me. You were left behind in the hospital.'

'Do you remember what that was like?' I asked.

There was a long pause. I could almost feel time stand still. 'Oh, Caitríona, it's very hard to get words to describe it. You feel as though you dreamt it all, that the whole thing was a dream. You felt it didn't happen. I cried for days afterwards. I did, I did.'

I was conscious of the agony that I was putting Sarah through, but I wanted more details: who was in the room, what was said, whether Sarah had sufficient time alone with me to say goodbye. But it became clear that Sarah had placed this memory at the furthest recess of her mind and locked it away. She reminded me of the survivors of the Srebrenica massacre I'd met, who often struggled to recall episodes of shattering distress. Lacking a clear recollection from Sarah, I am forced to rely on my own imagining. I see myself being wheeled away in my crib, bawling, wanting my mother. I see Sarah, still bleeding, her tender breasts leaking milk, bereft as she leaves the hospital.

In my childhood adoptee daydreams, Sarah had fought tooth and nail to keep me. It was painful to realize that this was not the case: there was never a moment when a phalanx of nurses and nuns struggled to remove me from her embrace. At the same time, I find it admirable that Sarah did not spin me a self-absolving line about her decision not to keep me. The odds were almost impossible: life in Ireland in 1972 as an unmarried mother, without the support of her family, would have been extraordinarily difficult. All this I understood. But the child in me wanted to hear that Sarah had put up a fight. The mother in me wanted to hear that too. Since giving birth to Liam and Caoimhe – marvelling at the physical torque on my heart when I first saw the faces of my newborn babies – I had struggled to comprehend Sarah's decision to give me away. Although the circumstances of our pregnancies had been miles apart, my experiences stoked an uncomfortable thought that refused to go away: that no woman, fully informed and left to her own devices, would make the decision Sarah had made.

Sarah returned to Anne and Paddy's house, took to her bed and cried for a couple of days. Then, with no one to counsel her, she decided to go home. A week or two back home, amongst her cheerful noisy siblings and the father she adored, would help her get her head back in order.

'Your instinct is to go home,' she told me that day in the Marine. 'I wanted to go home. I needed to.'

Sarah arrived to find her family still reeling in the wake of her mother's death. The house was chaotic, her father depressed. Teeming with hormones and sick with grief over her missing child, Sarah struggled to get through each day. She told her family she was off work because of the kidney infection. As far as she knew, nobody noticed her altered shape.

In reality, the secret was out. At Christmas, when Sarah had been just over five months pregnant, a neighbour had seen her and had her suspicions. Now, assessing her sagging midriff and pasty pallor, the neighbour put two and two together. Scandalized, she picked up the phone.

'The neighbour calls my aunt in Dublin and the aunt comes down,' Sarah recalled. 'I wasn't there. I know that all hell broke loose when she did come down. She and the neighbour told my father, instead of coming directly to me.'

'Where were you at that point?' I asked.

'I can't remember,' Sarah said. 'I honestly can't remember.'

Sarah has never been able to fully reconstruct for me the events immediately following her family's discovery that she had secretly given birth. There is, in her memory, no clear moment of truth, of confrontation, of renunciation. What I do know is that her father, devastated and shamed by his daughter's fall, would barely speak to her in the coming years and decades. She had brought dishonour on the household, she had stained the family name. Her relationship with her family as she had known it was over.

Now that the baby was gone, she could no longer lodge with Anne and Paddy. Although the medical certificate for her fictitious kidney infection protected her teaching position, she knew instinctively that she would never again set foot in that town. She would have to start over. There were more teaching jobs in Dublin than anywhere else, and the city's bustling anonymity seemed to suit her situation. But she could not afford lodgings in Dublin. There was only one person in Dublin with whom she could live rent-free: her aunt. The same aunt who had just betrayed her.

Even allowing for the financial and familial circumstances, it is hard to fathom how Sarah could have accepted the hospitality of this woman. Was there an element of self-punishment involved? Or perhaps just a sort of passivity that set in when, seeking to avoid stigma and scandal, she surrendered her autonomy and her baby?

In all the time I have known Sarah, she has never said anything unkind about anyone – with the sole exception of this aunt.

'She was a witch. She was very, very cruel. She would say anything.'

The aunt grudgingly told Sarah that she could remain at

her house throughout the summer until she found a new job and a place to live. In return, Sarah would have to live with her aunt's contempt, the disdain of the morally righteous for the fallen woman.

'Nobody will ever look at you again,' the aunt told Sarah one day. 'You're finished.'

'I believed her,' Sarah told me. 'I did. I really did.'

12

One morning in July 2014, while visiting Dublin, I outline to Liam and Mary my plans for the week.

'I'd like to drive out to Blackrock one afternoon,' I tell them. 'Just to take a look and see if the baby home in Temple Hill still exists.'

We are in the kitchen drinking tea. Sitting across from me beneath the picture of the Sacred Heart with the flickering red bulb, Mam regards me warily. Her eyes narrow as she pulls on a cigarette.

'What in God's name do you want to go back there for?' she asks. 'Sure that place is gone years ago.'

I pause, calibrating my response. I am painfully aware that my research risks pushing the limits of my parents' patience. I know that Liam and Mary are deeply concerned about the consequences of the book – for Sarah, for me, for us all. I wonder how much more they can take.

'It's just research,' I tell her. 'I'd like to describe what the building looks like, you know, to get a sense of the past. Why don't you come with me? We can stop in Eleanor's house on the way home.'

Two days later, on a hot afternoon, we drive out towards Blackrock in my rented car. It has taken a lot of cajoling to get Mam to come. A promise of lunch at the Tara Towers, a once-plush hotel to which Dad took business clients when we were young, has sealed the deal. I am grateful for the company. With little experience driving in Dublin, I have no clear idea where we're going, but Mam is adamant that she knows exactly where Temple Hill is.

Twenty-five minutes later we are in Blackrock. 'It should be here to the left,' Mam gestures suddenly as we pass an estate of red-brick houses near Blackrock village. 'Turn in here,' she points with her left hand, 'here.'

But I am too slow, and miss the turn. I continue along the main road, stopping further up to make a U-turn and approach again. I can't understand why Mam is insisting that we turn into a housing estate. I know for a fact that Temple Hill stood on its own acreage, surrounded by vast grounds. I'm convinced that Mam has it wrong, and I'm irritated by her certainty.

I make the turn again and enter the housing estate. All I see are tidy brick houses. I keep driving. Suddenly a large grey Georgian house looms into view. It has expansive bay windows and a cheerful red wooden door. From the photographs that I have studied, I recognize Temple Hill.

Mam, sitting to my left, gasps. I stop the car. 'It's still here,' she says, marvelling, leaning forward in her seat to get a better look.

I glance briefly at Mam and feel a sudden well of tears that is totally unexpected. I swallow hard.

'It looks just like it did the night we came to get you,' she says.

The telephone call came to Number 49 one afternoon in late May 1972. Mary answered and was told that she and Liam – and their older children, if they so desired – were to come to St Patrick's Infant Hospital, in Temple Hill, Blackrock, the following Friday evening at 7 p.m. sharp. Their new daughter had arrived.

Mary had already been to a haberdashery on St Stephen's Green to choose material to reupholster the Wilson Silver Cross pram that had served David. She had stripped the wallpaper in the bedroom she shared with Liam, and the two of them had repainted the borders and applied new rolls of pink and white paper. An elegant new crib had been purchased, delivered, assembled, and placed by Mary's side of the bed. Above the bed hung a wooden crucifix and a framed papal blessing. Opposite, two large wooden wardrobes stood sentry on either side of a pink-tiled fireplace. To the right was a large window that overlooked the back garden and the red-tiled roofs of the estate. The room was cosy, bright and welcoming, the perfect home for a new baby girl.

On Friday afternoon, 2 June, Mary made sure that Thérèse and David were scrubbed clean on their return from school, and Liam arrived home early from work. Suited up, their hair brushed, their shoes shining, the family ate a small teatime meal. Then, just before six o'clock – making ample allowance for Friday rush-hour traffic – they climbed into Liam and Mary's Hillman Imp. The air of expectation hung heavy in the car: Mary nervous and excited in the front, Thérèse and David silent and wide-eyed in the back. Liam, a cautious driver, kept his eyes on the road and on the clock.

In late February 2011, Dad and I boarded an early-morning train at Heuston station, Styrofoam cups of coffee and newspapers in hand. Ahead of us lay a four-hour journey to County Kerry. The previous month, trying to locate people who had worked at Temple Hill around the time I spent the first six weeks of my life there, I had come across a heading for 'St Patrick's Infant Hospital' on a reunion website; it took me a short while to work out that this was the place I knew as Temple Hill. The subheading was 'A hospital for babies for adoption and a college for Nursery Nurses run like a convent'. Through the site I had made contact with an Irishwoman, Lena Griffin, who lived in a village just outside of Tralee and who had worked as a trainee nurse at Temple Hill in the early 1970s. Lena told me she could remember it as if it was yesterday. What could she do to help?

I sat down and wrote a long email, filling in the background. I told her I was a journalist and that I was considering writing a book. I would be in Ireland the following month – perhaps I could pop down to Kerry to say hello?

The next day, a reply from Lena:

Lovely to hear from you. I'm sure your mother would love to tell everyone about you but guilt is an awful thing to have to live with, even though she has nothing to feel guilty about. It was the times we lived in. She wasn't the only one to have to give up her baby. When I think of all the little babies in Temple Hill it was so sad. It was so easy to get attached to them. Sometimes we would see the mothers bringing them in. All depended on the ward you were in at the time. Maybe this book will help your mother to release some of the guilt she holds inside? God help us, she wasn't the first and she certainly wasn't the last to have to give up her baby. I will gladly help in any way I can. How much help I'll be I don't know, but I will try my best.

A month later, sitting next to Dad on the train to Tralee, our newspapers spread before us and our elbows touching, I felt blissfully content. I hadn't anticipated having company on this trip, but on a whim the day before I had asked Dad if he wanted to tag along. He readily agreed to travel with me, suggesting that I visit Lena alone while he strolled around the town. Now, as the train slowed in its approach to Tralee, a weak February sun struggling through the winter light, I was glad for Dad's gentle presence. It seemed right, somehow, to have him along on this quest.

I knew only the barest facts about the six-week period between the end of my life with Sarah and the arrival of Liam and Mary at Temple Hill to adopt me. I knew that sometime on 21 April the car that was ferrying me from Holles Street to Temple Hill stopped briefly at St Andrew's Church on Westland Row – the same church, coincidentally, where Liam had been baptized forty-three years before. There, beneath the inscription *Ave Gratia Plena Dominus Tecum*, and in the arms of some woman who had agreed to act as a temporary godparent, I was held over the giant marble font and baptized. Father Dermot Clarke spoke the name that Sarah had given me two days before: Shona, a feminized version of her father's name.

I also had a first-hand memory of Temple Hill: not from when I was a newborn, but from 1979, when I was seven years old. Liam and Mary had brought me there on the Sunday of my First Holy Communion. I can remember climbing the steep granite stairs to the house, wearing my white dress and veil and clutching an enormous box of chocolates, a gift for the nun in charge. I can remember too a sea of female faces – some in religious veils and others with long nursing caps – swimming into view. The atmosphere was friendly, welcoming, and I was the star attraction. But later, clutching Liam's hand as we walked past rows and rows of squawking infants in an upstairs ward, I can remember feeling painfully sad and wanting to go home.

A couple of years ago, sitting with Liam and Mary over tea, I brought up this childhood visit to Temple Hill.

'Why did you bring me back there?' I asked. 'It felt weird at the time. It's a strange memory.'

Mam, somewhat defensively, was quick to respond. 'Sister

Angela, the head nun, she wanted to see you. She was interested in how you were getting on. We were just being courteous. Other friends who had adopted did the same.'

There was one other bit of information I had about Temple Hill: I knew from Palmer family lore that I had arrived at Number 49 on the night of 2 June 1972 with a nappy rash unlike anything my parents or neighbours had ever seen before, my tiny buttocks bleeding and raw. None of the solutions that Mary tried seemed to work. Finally, in desperation, Mam tracked down a paediatric specialist in a Dublin hospital. Over time, this doctor solved the rash. Even now, over forty years later while recounting the story, I can sense the terror my mother felt: she feared that if she couldn't sort out the rash, the nuns might take me away from her. But I had developed the rash at Temple Hill.

These were the thoughts in my mind as I exited the taxi outside Lena's house and approached her neat front garden. Could she shed light on what my life as a newborn would have been like for those weeks in the spring of 1972? I rang the bell and watched through the glass as a tall, thin woman with short hair emerged into the narrow hallway. As I had on my visit to Temple Hill thirty-two years before, I clutched a large box of chocolates. Lena smiled brightly when she saw me and pulled back her sliding porch door to let me in: 'Come in out of the cold,' she said. 'You're very welcome.'

Lena Griffin places a tray of coffee and biscuits on a low table in front of me in her living room. Sitting down on the couch adjacent to my armchair, she reaches across to pick up a packet of cigarettes.

'I hope you don't mind?' she asks in her Kerry lilt as she clicks on a cigarette lighter, takes a pull and exhales.

I smile and nod my consent, taking a sip of my coffee. It

seems like a good time to begin. 'I thought I'd start by asking how you first heard about Temple Hill?'

'It was a friend of mine, she told me about it,' Lena says. 'I was working in a small shop in town at the time. She said to me, "Shall we go to Dublin to do nursing?" But I don't think we realized what it would be like, what a strict regime it would be. I was there from about October 1973 to April 1975. I was about seventeen when I went.

'I don't think I knew, going up to Dublin, what type of children's nursing I would be doing. I thought it was just a hospital for sick children. I didn't realize that it was a home for babies. It took a while for the penny to drop before I knew what I was there for. It was shocking to me because I never realized there would be so many babies given away like that.'

Next to Lena on the couch sit three frayed colour photographs. She picks them up and hands them to me. 'I dug these out before you came,' she says. 'They're the only ones I have of that time.'

My heart skips a beat. The first photo shows a young woman in a short-sleeved blue nursing uniform, a wide white belt at her waist and a long white nursing veil. She sits on an armchair, her legs crossed, and regards the camera warily. A white plastic name tag with a red background is pinned above her heart.

'That's me in the sitting room at Temple Hill. After work we'd sit there for a couple of hours in the evening. We'd work from eight to eight. It was always busy. We were constantly going, we never stopped. Even if you did stop you'd probably be caught because there was always someone watching.' Lena laughs ruefully at the memory. 'There were glass panels in the ward. The ward sisters would be passing and looking in all the time. Sister Francis Lombard was the nun in charge.

We used to call her "Fanny", that was the nickname we'd use. "Fanny's coming," we'd say, and then we would scatter. If you were caught talking – and often we were – God, you'd be kicked back down.'

She hands me the second photograph. Two young women in nursing uniforms, sitting on low stools. Each holds a baby in her arms. In the background sits a large plastic tub filled with water and a cast-iron radiator painted in the same ugly mustard tone as the wall behind it. Above the radiator hang silky curtains with a garish floral print. I cannot take my eyes off the babies, who are dressed in white calico gowns. The larger of the two, sitting on the lap of a young nurse wearing large glasses, is arching his back and crying. He looks about six months old. The other baby is much smaller, with blonde hair and delicate features. She sits wide-eyed in the crook of the other nurse's left arm, her tiny mouth slightly agape with wonder. She is heartbreakingly beautiful.

'We got up at seven, we ate breakfast at half seven and we were in the ward at eight. The night nurses would give their report before they went off. And then we went straight to cleaning, polishing the floors, the windows, the doors, the whole lot. We bathed the babies at 10 a.m. We would pull screens around and fill the baths with water. It would all be done on your lap. You'd wash their hair first, over the bath, then you'd dry their hair. Then you'd take their nappy off and bathe them. You'd put a little bit of Vaseline behind their ears. You'd use little bits of cotton wool to clean inside their ears. And then you'd powder their necks and blow the excess powder off.'

I smile at the level of detail that Lena is offering, imagining these young nurses with their tiny charges, large billowy clouds of talcum powder hovering in the air.

'We sat on stools at a table to feed the babies. That's when we would get a chance to chat amongst ourselves. We fed the babies every four hours. No feeding on demand. If they were sound asleep you'd have to wake them. They might only take an ounce and then they'd be asleep again. There's no way that you can feed a child that doesn't want it. But then we'd have to get rid of the extra three ounces. You'd be caught if the child cried two hours later looking for the rest of its bottle that you'd already dumped. You'd be reported for that.'

'What do you mean "reported"?' I ask.

'We wrote reports on everything. Let's say if a child brought up milk from the previous feed – that meant they hadn't been properly winded from the feed before. You'd have to report that. If it happened when I was feeding a baby I wouldn't report it, unless one of the staff nurses were there and saw it, because you'd be getting your friends in trouble. At 6 p.m. every day we would have to go downstairs with our lists and report whether the babies ate well, if one had been sick, if their stools were loose or not. It was a written report and we would have to call it out to Sister Francis. The head staff nurse would be there as well. They wore a white uniform. Sister Francis, too. She had a large crucifix round her neck.'

The day sounds frenetic and rushed, I suggest. Was there ever any time to linger over the babies?

Lena pauses. She furrows her brow in thought. 'You'd hold them every now and then but you wouldn't have much time for it. Feed it, change it, get up its wind and bathe it.'

She frowns with the memory. 'Then you'd just move on to the next.'

That conversation with Lena was an unexpected gift. By the time I returned to Tralee to meet Dad, I had taken a virtual tour through the corridors of the hospital in the 1970s. I could picture the ground floor of Temple Hill and the formal office just off the entryway where adoptive parents would come to wait. I could visualize the admissions ward next door where the babies lived before being transferred upstairs to the main wards: St Theresa's, St Joseph's, St Agnes's and St Michael's. I learned that the bigger kids – children as old as three and four years old, some with disabilities – slept in St Michael's. The littlest were housed in tiny cubicles in St Agnes's, which doubled up as a training ward for the young nursing recruits. Nearby was a sluice room where dirty cloth nappies were rinsed in buckets before being sent to the laundry. Across the way was a kitchen where trainees mixed up bottles of infant formula, tagged them individually, placed them in rattling metal containers and dispatched them to the wards.

A year and a half after my meeting with Lena, my inbox yielded a surprise email via the reunion website, this time from a woman living in the United Kingdom named Hilary Piper. 'I worked at Temple Hill from 72–74,' she wrote. 'I was very young, 15 years old when I started, and may not have a lot of information, but I am more than happy to share anything with you.'

I called Hilary from the little office overlooking the cherry tree in the front yard of our home in Washington. She answered on the second ring, in the accent of the West Country of England, where she had been living for the past few decades. I liked the sound of Hilary's voice immediately. She came across as forthright and sincere, eager to help.

'We had a local newspaper called the *Dundalk Democrat* that we always got on a Saturday,' Hilary told me over the phone that day. 'My mother would go into town on a bus to shop and she would bring back the newspaper. I was due to leave school and was looking through the paper. There was a photograph of a girl from Dundalk in her uniform who had just finished at Temple Hill and was going to be a nanny in a private house. I saw this picture and thought, "That's something that I would really like to do." And so I wrote to Temple Hill and that was that. My parents were pleased that I was stepping out to do something that was different. But I had no idea. It was described as a dietetic hospital. I believed that the babies had eating problems. I honestly did.'

An image of Sister Francis floated into my mind: 'Can you remember any of the staff?' I asked.

'Sister Francis was in charge. She was very strict. She'd line us up at the start of each shift to ensure that our uniform was as it should be. If you had any hair showing from under your veil, a mark on your shoes or a ladder in your tights, Sister Francis would either stop your half day or take money out of your wages. I can remember her lifting my dress up to make sure that there wasn't a ladder in my tights higher than the knee. Anything you did wrong was punishable. There was a lot of fear.

'My name back then was McDonnell. And they would just refer to you using your surname. If there were people around, prospective parents, it would be "Nurse". Otherwise they would just shout, "McDonnell, fold those nappies."' After a pause, Hilary laughed: 'We folded a lot of nappies.'

Hilary's account matched what I'd heard from Lena: the drudgery of twelve-hour shifts, snatches of illicit conversations while feeding the babies, the fear of Sister Francis and of selling out their peers.

What about the care for the babies? Were they well looked after?

'Yes, I think the babies were well cared for,' Hilary said. 'I can remember once a young nurse being a bit rough with a baby in frustration because the baby wouldn't stop crying, but that's the only incident I can remember of somebody being a bit nasty. But when you look back, we were just young girls who had come straight from school with very little education. We did the best we could. But whether that was good enough? There is a big question mark over that.'

I told Hilary about my nappy rash, and recounted what Lena had told me about the daily routine.

'We were on a set schedule and a routine,' Hilary agreed. 'We had to make sure that everything was done according to the timescale. And so if you fed a baby, put it back down and it soiled its nappy then it was going to be in it for quite some time.

'There was no spontaneity or acknowledging an individual baby's needs. They were on the conveyer belt, basically, and there was no stepping off it.'

But despite the drudgery of the assembly line, there were moments of hilarity. Like the time Sister Francis was called to the wards in the middle of the night and arrived without her habit, her head exposed. 'She was nearly bald,' Hilary told me, laughing. 'It was the greatest source of entertainment to us. We laughed about it for months. We went from calling her Sister Fanny to Sister Baldie. We just loved it! It was the greatest victory.'

So too were the unexpected moments of pleasure: a cake to celebrate a nurse's birthday, the chance to catch a double-decker bus into Dublin city, hearing Ringo Starr singing 'You're Sixteen' on the wireless inadvertently left on in a ward.

'We used to steal chocolate from the vending machine,' Hilary said. 'We learned very early on that if there was two of us and we stood on either side and shook it, the chocolate

would come out. We used to also go to a little shop in the village called Meany's and buy crisps and sweets and lemonade.
Then we'd sit in our rooms in the evening and just eat. When
you think back on it, it was slave labour really. We got certificates and badges but in the end it didn't stack up to much.'

I asked Hilary whether she eventually worked out the true
nature of the institution.

She sighed. 'It took an awful long time for me to realize. I
came from the country. I had never left home. The whole
thing was a huge culture shock for me. I thought that the
babies we were looking after were babies that were ill. I didn't
realize that they were up for adoption. I think finally some of
the older trainees passed the information down. The nuns or
staff nurses never discussed it with us. When I look back, I
can remember Sister Francis coming around with prospective parents. She was on the ball and would whip everyone
into shape. The place had to be like a new pin and the babies
had to be presented. When I look back at that now, it's horrible. It's almost like putting out sweets in a shop. Who is
going to have the biggest bar? Who is going to have the
whitest chocolate?'

'And were you aware of the babies arriving from the
maternity hospitals?'

'No, they would just turn up. If you were on night duty
you would go off in the morning and come back in the evening and there'd be two, maybe three new babies. We never
questioned it.'

'And what about when they left?'

'You would come in for your shift and they would be gone.
They seemed to do it at night, during the handover between
the day and night shift. I never remember a couple coming
into a ward and being handed a baby. It seemed to be done
out of sight.'

I made a mental note. Liam and Mary were instructed to be at Temple Hill at 7 p.m., enough time for Sister Francis to hear the daily reports from the wards at 6 p.m. and to then clear the corridors of the bulk of her nursing staff.

'And when you look back,' I said, 'what are your thoughts about the whole experience? How do you feel?'

Hilary sighed. 'I feel a huge amount of sadness. A huge amount of sadness to think I didn't know. And to wonder whether if I had known could I have made a difference? At fifteen, probably not. I didn't have enough education, I didn't have enough knowledge. I suppose, in a way, the experience did spur me on to do something more constructive with my life. That's why I became a social worker.'

There was one question I'd forgotten to ask.

'By the way, when I was seven, my parents took me back to Temple Hill when I made my First Communion. Did you ever see any other kids returning like that?'

'All the time,' Hilary said. 'I remember children coming in dressed in their First Communion outfits. It must have been something that Fanny would have said to the new parents: "Oh, do come back and show her to us when she's made her First Communion."'

Hilary paused. 'It's almost as if she was saying, "You belong to us."'

While Liam, Mary, Thérèse and David waited to meet me for the first time in the office adjacent to the admissions ward on the ground floor of Temple Hill, tea and biscuits were served and glasses of warm orange squash for the kids. Eventually, at around 7.30 p.m., Sister Angela brought me into the room. I was placed into Mary's outstretched arms. My parents could not believe their eyes: a beautiful new daughter, neatly pack-aged and delivered, just like that.

According to my family, I screamed all the way home from Temple Hill. Nothing Mary did could soothe me.

At the approach to O'Connell Bridge, Liam had a sudden thought. Not wanting to spoil the moment, he kept it to himself. But eventually, as my cries filled the air, Liam decided to speak his mind.

'I remember saying in the car as we passed Amiens Street train station, "I wonder if she knows?"' Dad told me once, some time ago, about that moment. 'I wondered whether you knew. Whether you could sense that we were taking you away.'

13

In June 1972, lodging miserably in her aunt's house in Dublin, Sarah scanned the employment notices in the daily newspapers. That month, the papers were full of stories about the case of a twenty-seven-year-old Irish woman, Mary McGee, who had sought a declaration in the High Court of Ireland over the seizure by customs officials of contraceptives that she purchased overseas. McGee, a mother of four with a heart condition, suffered complications in her previous pregnancies and doctors told her that she risked her life were she to have another child. Unable to buy contraceptives in Ireland, McGee ordered spermicidal jelly from the United Kingdom, but the product was seized by vigilant Irish customs officials. She decided to take a legal challenge to the seizure, a gutsy crusade by a suburban Dublin mother. At one point under cross-examination, a barrister asked McGee's husband, James, whether he and his wife 'would not consider living as brother and sister'.

I was too shy to ask Sarah point-blank whether she and Tom used contraception, but on one occasion I asked whether she knew if contraception was available back then.

'I'm sure it was but I didn't know,' Sarah said. 'At the time I was so gullible. I didn't really know about the pill or condoms. But I should have known better.'

In the early 1970s, enterprising lovers had to cross the border into Northern Ireland if they wanted to buy a packet of condoms, and I doubted whether Tom had ever made that trip. In May 1971, a year before Mary McGee would take her case to the High Court, a group of forty-nine women had caused embarrassment to the Irish government by taking a train from Dublin to Belfast and returning later that day to brandish condoms and contraceptive jelly in the faces of customs officials at the terminus. Mary McGee would prevail in her petition to the High Court, securing a ruling that the ban on the importation of contraceptives for personal use was unconstitutional and that the state had intruded on her marital privacy. But it was not until 1979 that the Irish government finally introduced legislation to decriminalize contraception. This bill was, in the words of the then Minister for Health, Charles Haughey, 'an Irish solution to an Irish problem', permitting married couples to access contraceptives with a prescription, while allowing doctors and pharmacists who had moral objections to refuse to handle the offending materials. Irish people would have to wait until 1994 – the year following my graduation from university – before contraception became freely available.

The winds of change represented by Mary McGee and the 'contraceptive train' meant little to Sarah, living with her disapproving aunt. Feminism might have been on the march, but the women in Sarah's world – the suspicious neighbour in her home village, the busybody aunt in Dublin – had conspired to punish her for stepping out of line. Why should Sarah get away with her reprehensible behaviour when others had avoided sex outside of marriage? 'If you want to get people to behave, show what happens to those who don't,' an Irish historian once said to me about Ireland's culture of female surveillance and the institutionalization of unmarried mothers. 'Make them feel part of that punishment.' Her aunt's verdict – *Nobody will ever look at you again. You're finished* – echoed constantly in Sarah's mind.

There was one person that summer who did show her

unexpected kindness: a nun in a Dublin school who offered Sarah a teaching position for the upcoming September term.

'I was very lucky,' Sarah told me. 'I just called in person to the school and the principal was very kind. She gave me a job, there and then.'

Although Sarah's recent absence from teaching for nearly all of the previous school year must have looked fairly dubious, the nun didn't ask any questions. 'I think she might have guessed my situation,' Sarah told me. 'But she never said anything.'

Sarah began work that September determined to start afresh. But, as hard as she tried, she could not forget my long limbs, my black hair, how natural it had felt to hold me in her arms. At night, tormented by recurrent, distressing flashbacks to her pregnancy and my birth, Sarah began to suffer anxiety attacks. As she stood in front of her new class, my face would often swim into view, causing her stomach to lurch with grief and longing. She spent most of her free time wondering where I was, imagining some other woman holding me, feeding me. From now on she would live each day as two separate people: the teacher, keeping it all together; and the secret mother, grief-stricken, who would never again feel whole.

'You go through the motions but something has died in you,' Sarah told me once. 'You're two people. You're two people and you're on the run, basically. You're on the run for evermore.'

The legislation that governed my adoption by Liam and Mary came into force on 1 January 1953. In the preceding decades, particularly during the 1940s, various Irish charities and voluntary organizations – concerned about the alarmingly high death rate among illegitimate infants, the overcrowding in mother-and-baby homes and the flow of Irish babies to adoptive parents overseas, especially to the USA, and often in exchange for significant sums of money – issued repeated calls to legalize adoption. De facto adoptive parents across Ireland were anxious to legitimize their relationship with their non-biological children, many of whom lacked any official documentation, and to ensure that these children were offered legal protection. A letter sent by an adoptive mother to the office of the Taoiseach in 1950 urged the government to introduce legislation. 'Please get on with it now . . . My boy has no idea that he is not our very own flesh and blood . . . he is now at school and we must produce this birth certificate shortly.'

But the Church hierarchy continued to resist all government measures to introduce legal adoption. Adoption had never been doctrinally incompatible with Catholicism, but in Ireland there was a pervasive fear that legalized adoption might allow Catholic babies to find their way into Protestant homes. While researching at the Dublin Archdiocese's archives in 2011, I came across countless documents discussing this problem, some written in the distinctive spidery script of the long-serving Archbishop of Dublin, John Charles McQuaid.

One document, addressed to McQuaid and dated 21 October 1951, outlined the findings of an episcopal subcommittee commissioned to review the proposed legislation for adoption.

> The sub-committee is of the opinion that the Church has a legitimate interest in the terms of any Adoption Act: (a) in so far as its operation might constitute a danger to the faith of Catholics and particularly of Catholic children . . . Two dangers may be apprehended here: (a) the danger that Catholic children, or children who should be Catholics, might be

adopted by non-Catholics and brought up in a non-Catholic religion, and (b) a danger that Catholics, and particularly unmarried Catholic mothers, might be induced to change their religion in order to make a particular adoption possible.

In the end, McQuaid prevailed: personally poring over every last line of the draft legislation and ensuring that his hand-picked subcommittee scrutinized every clause before it was finally introduced in parliament. As enacted, the law ensured that a child could be adopted only by people of the same faith. It also made it impossible for the birth mother to trace the child.

The daylight had not yet waned when Liam finally pulled into the driveway of Number 49 on 2 June 1972. I was still crying, my lusty wails signalling to the neighbours that the Palmers were home.

'We got home at about 9 p.m.,' Mam remembers. 'It was still bright and sunny. All the kids were out on the street. Mona, who had already adopted two little boys, brought them over to welcome you. And then Noreen came over. And Teresa. And Máire from next door.'

I imagine the scene: the excitement in the house, the *oohs* and *aahs* of our neighbours echoing around the living room, the pride on Mary's face.

Half an hour later I was bundled up again and taken next door into Number 51, the home of Bríd and Fergus, the loving couple who became like a second set of parents to me. Although it was late, Anne, their five-year-old daughter, was still awake, having been allowed to stay up for this special occasion.

I was still crying. Anne, now feeling the effects of being up two hours past her bedtime, was unimpressed by the fuss. Ceremoniously, Fergus took me in his arms and kneeled before his youngest child so she could assess the bundle at eye level. Anne peered inside, considered her newest playmate and scrunched up her nose. She turned to Bríd with disgust.

'You kept me up for that?'

On the morning of 3 June, a little over twelve hours after my arrival, Mary remembers watching a large van pull up outside Number 49.

'About ten nuns came out of a van, including Sister Dympna, Sister Brendan, Sister Eleanor and Sister Brenda,' Mam told me, still laughing at the memory. 'Your dad had been helping them with a musical at the school. They all arrived out to see the Palmers' new arrival.'

Two weeks later I was taken to the local church in Raheny and once again suspended over a baptismal font. My extended family, my godparents Noleen and Jack King, and our closest neighbours formed a tight circle round Liam and Mary. The ceremony was a sham – the Catholic Church does not allow an individual to be baptized twice – but it was important for Liam and Mary to publicly christen me as their own. I was no longer Shona, the daughter of Sarah. I was now Caitríona, their child in name.

I have three photographs from that day, taken in the back garden of Number 49. In each photo I am a sleeping bundle, swathed in heirloom christening robes and held tightly in the arms of the female triumvirate that would nurture and protect me throughout my childhood: my mother, Mary, our next-door neighbour Bríd and my beloved godmother Noleen. Mary, dressed in powder blue, looks joyous and elegant as she holds me in the crook of her right arm. Nestled against her, beaming, are Thérèse and David. To the left of Mary stands Liam, smartly attired in his best brown suit, his shoulders back, his chest puffed out.

Despite this ceremonial induction into the Palmer clan, my first months with my adoptive family unfolded under a probationary shadow. Sister Angela's spot checks on the house did not end when St Patrick's Guild judged Mary and Liam fit parents. Early one Monday morning, as Thérèse and David ran wild through the house and a mountain of laundry lay piled on the kitchen floor, the telephone rang: it was Sister Angela, saying she was on her way out to the house. Mam ran next door to Bríd, who mobilized Thérèse and her daughters Claire and Mary on cleaning duty, and got to work baking scones in her own kitchen. For her part, Mam turned to the pile of laundry sitting on the kitchen floor. She stuffed as much of it as she could into the washing machine and then threw the rest into a large black refuse bag, pushing it into the furthest recess of the tiny cloakroom beneath the stairwell. Back in the kitchen, her attention was suddenly drawn to a row of cloth nappies fluttering on the clothes line in the garden. Still struggling to solve my nappy rash, Mary had been applying a topical antifungal solution to my buttocks, a product known as Gentian Violet. The solution contained a strong antiseptic dye and the nappies were now stained a vivid purple.

'I had put a line of nappies out the night before and they were dry,' Mam recalled. 'But they were all stained with this Gentian Violet. Bríd said, "Here, give them to me." And I said, "No, here's what I'll do. I'll stick them down behind the boiler." And I did.'

The image of my mother on her hands and knees in the upstairs bathroom of Number 49 furtively stuffing purple-stained nappies behind the large copper water boiler always makes me smile. But there was real fear behind it. In Mam's mind, she could lose me over the most frivolous thing, including a clothes line of discoloured nappies. She wasn't taking any chances.

'Angela shows up and the first thing she did was to sniff the air and say, "Such a gorgeous smell of baking." She did the rounds of the house and asked to check on you. Later, sitting there with a cup of tea and a scone, she said to me, "You're a great woman to be baking at this hour of the morning, Mrs Palmer."'

Mary and Liam's deeper worry in those early months arose from the fact that I could not yet be officially called their child. The adoption legislation specified that an adoption order could not be made before the child was six months old; it also specified that the consent of the birth mother could be 'withdrawn at any time before the making of an adoption order'. Still in need of a hysterectomy but delaying the surgery until the adoption papers were signed, Mary was on edge.

On 18 October, one day before I would reach the official eligibility age for adoption, a letter arrived from St Patrick's Guild. The letter requested that Liam and Mary submit three health certificates proving our collective good health and officially inform St Patrick's Guild of my chosen name. The following morning, Liam by her side, Mary placed me in my pram and pushed me round the corner to the family doctor, Patrick O'Brien. The surgery would not be open until 3 that afternoon, but Mary was determined not to wait. Thirty minutes later she emerged with two health certificates, both dated 19 October 1972 and signed by Dr O'Brien. The first was about me: *This is to certify that the above baby has been examined by me and is in perfect health and no abnormalities were detected.* The second was about Liam and Mary: *This is to certify that in my opinion the above patients are in perfect physical and mental health.*

Back at Number 49, Liam placed the two health certificates in an envelope and enclosed a handwritten note:

Liam and Mary had jumped through all the necessary
hoops. All that remained, they believed, were formalities.
But as October turned to November, there was no word
from St Patrick's Guild about the making of an adoption
order. Mary, worried, contacted Sister Angela. The nun, at
first evasive, finally told her that she had been unable to
make contact with 'the mother' to get her signature on the
documentation. Mam recalled, 'She told us that your mother
was a young school teacher who had gotten involved with
another school teacher and that she had fled to London
after she gave you up. That's all that we knew. We didn't
question it.'

The London story was a lie. Neither Sarah nor my parents can understand why St Patrick's Guild promulgated this
falsehood. Sarah was not in London but just a few miles
away in Dublin, trying to rebuild her shattered life. She woke
up every morning focused on just one thought: get through
the day. The simplest tasks were endurance tests of epic
proportions. She barely had enough energy to make it across
the city to work each day, let alone to 'flee' to London. She
is adamant that she never heard from St Patrick's Guild during this time.

That year, my first Christmas at Number 49, I was inun-
dated with more presents than any baby needs. The house
teemed with visitors. 'Any word yet on the papers?' Liam

and Mary were constantly asked as I was passed round from relative to relative.

And then, on 27 December, a belated and unexpected Christmas gift for the family: a phone call from Sister Angela to say that Sarah had finally been located and the papers signed. The adoption could at last be formalized. Sister Angela did not offer any more details and Mary, deeply curious but anxious not to rock the boat, decided not to ask.

Six weeks later, on 6 February 1973, Thérèse and David were given a day off school, dressed once again in their Sunday best and placed in the back of the Hillman Imp. Chomping on a bottle and head to toe in lacy frills, I rode with Liam and Mary up front.

'I remember that room so clearly. It was so formal,' Thérèse recalled of their destination, the office of the Irish Adoption Board on Merrion Square. 'It was very dark with a big board table.'

The formalities took a few minutes: the reading of the adoption order, the confirmation of names, dates and places of birth, and the reaffirmed willingness of the Palmer family to make this infant child their own. Then, with the flourish of my parents' signatures, the fear and waiting were over. Handshakes all round, pats on the head for my older siblings.

Later that month, on 19 February, Liam and Mary received a final letter from St Patrick's Guild. It was a brief note attached to another page, a badly typed document labelled 'Particulars of Adoption Order'. Marked 'confidential', the document noted my date of birth, the name Sarah had given me, her name, and, in the space for the birth father, two crooked lines marked 'XXXXXX'. Now the state and baptismal registers that had been drawn up in the wake of my birth and my shotgun baptism on 22 April would be superseded by new documents that made no reference to my biological mother.

At the Marine Hotel in February 2011, I ask Sarah if she can remember signing the adoption papers and whether she felt fully informed as to the finality of that act.

'I think I went to the St Patrick's Guild office on O'Connell Street to sign the papers. But then again . . .' She pauses. 'You're so traumatized that your mind plays tricks on you . . . When you are in that position you need somebody with you to advocate for you. But I was alone.'

On a bookshelf in my home in Washington sits a slim red book that a friend, a professor at a local university, found recently in the depths of his campus library. The book, *Adoption: The Parent, The Child, The Home*, was written by Monsignor Cecil J. Barrett, CC, long recognized as the architect of Ireland's adoption law, and published in 1952. The cover features a small child, frowning slightly, who stands in a crib with his arms outstretched. Cecil Barrett's name popped up countless times in my trawl through the diocesan archives. As the head of the Catholic Social Welfare Bureau in the early 1950s, his fingerprints were all over the hierarchy's attempts to shape adoption legislation.

The book contains countless references to the unmarried 'girl' – her 'fall', her 'occasion of sin', her 'rehabilitation', her 'self-gratification' and 'lust'. I open a random page in a chapter titled 'The Mother'.

And so it is that she makes her final decision and offers her child for adoption . . . She knows that she will never see her child again, that she will never know him and that he will never know his mother. It is not easy for her, but she decides to make the sacrifice for the sake of her child. She believes she is doing the right thing by entrusting her little one to the care of others who will give him love and affection, and provide him with a good home, adequate education and a good Catholic upbringing. She could not provide these herself, and so she finds consolation in her distress in the belief that her child will be better off and his future more secure. The agency will not divulge to her the identity of her child's adoptive parents, because experience has shown that such knowledge tends to keep her unsettled. She may feel anxious to see for herself how her child is progressing and she may pay furtive visits to the locality in which the adoptive parents reside, in the hope of seeing her child. She may find it impossible to forget and, regretting the past so much, she may lose interest in the future. The adoptive parents would not wish that their identity should be known to the mother for they would live in dread that she might return one day and take her child away from them.

The agency, while not telling her where the child is, will encourage her to keep in touch and she will be informed of the child's progress in his new home. After a few months the majority of mothers are not heard of again: they have begun to make a fresh start, satisfied that the agency and the adoptive parents will carefully look after the child's future.

I read these passages and I think of Sarah. I imagine her back in January 1973 and try to inhabit her experience. How must it have felt to be offered a contract for a second chance – the chance to begin with a clean slate, to return to work, to find love again, to marry – on the condition that she surrender her child? For Sarah – and so many other young women like her – giving up a child for adoption must have felt a little like brokering a deal with the devil. It was rather like putting a Catholic twist on the old Grimm fairy tale,

Rumpelstiltskin: give me your child, your soul, and I will eradicate your shame.

In February 2011, over two days in the Marine Hotel, I interviewed Sarah for this book. She told me that in the months and years that followed my adoption she found herself drawn to playgrounds and parks, haunted by the faces of random children, forced to do a double take any time she passed a little girl with a shock of black hair.

'I could have sworn that I saw you a couple of times, in a buggy, on a street,' she told me. 'You'd see a child with loads of dark hair and your heart would stop.'

Sarah began to look forward to the beginning of every new school term, waiting for the moment when she could scroll through the student registry and scan the list of new students. 'I was always checking the roll books, always looking for your date of birth, always wondering if you were in the school.'

The extreme anxiety that enveloped Sarah eventually became a persistent and dull depression, an achy heaviness that hummed inside from the moment she opened her eyes to when she closed them again at night.

The days passed, one after another, the heaviness always there. 'It's like having a huge weight on your head. There's no joy. There's an edge to everything. Even on a nice day. You look out the window and it's a nice day but inside something is bothering you. No matter what, you're always ducking and diving.'

By the early 1980s, Sarah had met another man. He was sweet-natured and kind, and from a rural background much like hers. Fearful and cautious, barely daring to let herself breathe, Sarah gradually allowed herself to fall in love. But it all seemed too good to be true. Unlike Tom, this new man,

Michael, delighted in his beautiful girlfriend and wanted to show her off. He was courteous, principled, a man of his word. Soon, Michael was talking marriage and Sarah was on edge. She needed to tell him, she *wanted* to tell him, but every time she drew breath to utter the necessary words, her courage failed. *I'll do it tomorrow*, she would think. *The next day. The day after that.* Fearful that she would lose her one chance at happiness, she never did it. *No one will ever look at you again*, she heard her aunt say. *You're finished.*

'If I had come out and said it in the beginning, it would have made life so much easier. But I knew he would walk away if I did. I knew he would have walked away.'

'How do you know?' I asked.

'I just know. And so I just went headlong into it. We married. I hadn't told him. And before you know it years had passed and I still hadn't told him. Fear makes you do awful things.'

I do not know Sarah's husband. I have never met him or even seen his photograph. But from what Sarah has told me, I have some sense of this man. He seems kind, a devoted father and husband, a genuinely good person. But he is also, from what Sarah has told me, a religious man and Ireland at that time was a deeply conservative society. Sarah had already suffered the breakdown of her relationship with her beloved father, a man who had adored her. Disclosing my existence to Michael was just too great a risk.

Cecil Barrett, for his part, had an interesting take on this question:

Should a girl who has been offered marriage by another man, tell him about baby? In general, the answer is this: Firstly, she is not bound to tell him: she is entitled to her good name and reputation and she is under no obligation to tell him of any previous lapse from virtue. Secondly, prudence might demand that she should tell him. If he were to learn of the truth from an outsider after marriage, the happiness of their marriage might be seriously endangered. In each particular case, it would always be wiser to advise the girl to consult her Confessor on this delicate question.

Sarah did not go to confession for this matter. Instead, she had her own internal conscience to excoriate her every day: *You have to tell him. When will you tell him? The longer you wait the worse it will be.* But there was never a good time. She and Michael were married. Within a year of the wedding, Sarah was pregnant. She pretended to her husband, his family, her friends and neighbours that this was her first pregnancy, acting as though every pain, every twinge, every hint of nausea was a novelty she was experiencing for the first time. Keeping up the lie was exhausting, overwhelming.

'Fear, fear, fear,' she told me. 'I was dying inside.'

When Sarah went into labour, Michael drove her to the hospital but opted, as was common back then, to wait outside the delivery suite. Sarah was relieved. For the first time in over a decade, she came clean, confessing to the midwives on duty that this was her second pregnancy, not her first; that she had surrendered her first child for adoption.

I once asked Sarah if her second labour had been as easy as her first.

She shook her head vehemently. 'I found it so hard because I was reliving your whole birth . . . I found the whole birth very traumatic.'

'Was it a relief that this baby was a boy?' I suggested. 'Would it have been harder had it been a girl?'

'Probably. But I didn't care. I just wanted to have it over with.'

The secret only became more toxic as the years passed.

'Nothing was right. I made things worse and worse as the years went by. It just got bigger, and bigger, and bigger. I felt as though I was acting all the time, just going through the motions. Half of my head would be doing what I was supposed to be doing, and the other half would be full of everything that had happened. It's still like that all the time. I am always reliving the whole thing. I feel as though nothing is right. I feel as though I have totally messed up.'

To cope with the strain of this double life, Sarah put me in a box that she placed in the furthest reaches of her mind. Sometimes at night, when the kids were in bed, she would find refuge in her bedroom. There she would unpack me from the box, lift me out into the light, allow her mind to wander, luxuriating in thoughts of me.

'You were in my head. I was enjoying you in my head. I felt as if I had you all to myself. I would just remove myself from everyone and go upstairs for an hour to think about you. In my fantasy world I felt as though you were enjoying life. I hoped you were. I imagined you going through all the stages of primary school, secondary school, everything. All the different stages. There wasn't a day where I didn't think about you. I thought about you every day. Every day.'

'What about on my birthday?' I asked, thinking of the dread that I felt every year in the approach to 19 April. Often, I would act out on that day, sabotaging my birthday party, pouting and sulking like a spoilt brat. In retrospect, I realize that I was being forced to celebrate a time of devastating personal loss.

'Oh, that was a tough day,' Sarah said, dropping her gaze. 'That was a very tough day. I dreaded them. I really did. I would be very, very, very low on those days.'

I looked out of the window. Heavy grey clouds were stretched low across the sea, and here and there long shafts of light illuminated the green of Dublin Bay. Growing up, I used to watch on cloudy days for these columns of sunlit air, believing that they were God's way of transporting a recently departed soul.

I turned to Sarah. There was a question I had been wanting to ask her for years: 'Did you ever think of suicide?'

Sarah looked at me. 'I often think of suicide,' she said.

She noticed the look of horror on my face and reached across to me. 'But I won't do it. Don't worry,' she said, running her hand up and down my arm. 'I couldn't hurt my kids. I couldn't hurt any of them. They'd be there waiting for me to come home.'

I felt from her a fathomless sadness, a crushing weight.

'We'd *all* be there waiting for you,' I told her. 'You know that, don't you? How much we love you? All of us?'

14

January 2014

Dan and I are having dinner at the home of a friend, an Irish diplomat living in Washington. At the end of the evening, as we are saying goodbye, my friend takes me aside to tell me that Philomena Lee will be visiting Washington that week.

'Do you want me to send you the contacts for her publicity people?' he asks. 'Given your own story, it would be wonderful if you could meet her.'

I accept my friend's offer, but don't have the heart to tell him that I have yet to see the hit movie about Philomena's search for the son she was forced to give up for adoption in Ireland in the early 1950s. Nor have I read the book on which it is based, by Martin Sixsmith, a journalist who helped Philomena in her search. The story hits way too close to home. When I saw the film trailer I was weeping within the first ten seconds.

Three days later I enter the lobby of the Ritz Carlton hotel on M Street. I am met by a PR woman, clipboard in hand, who crosses my name off a list. She is elegantly dressed and supremely officious.

'We're running a little behind. You're the last of the day. Philomena is very tired so I'm afraid you'll have to be quick. You can sit there and wait while they finish up with their current interview.'

I sit in a corner and check the battery level on my tape recorder. I feel nervous, because there may be more to this meeting than the article I will write. Like Sarah, Philomena married and had children after giving up her first child for adoption. Like Sarah, she kept the story of her lost child a secret from her husband and kids for decades. Perhaps she can help me peer inside Sarah's mind?

A door to my left opens and a familiar face emerges. It is Mari Steed, a well-known advocate for Magdalen survivors and within Irish adoption circles. Mari is a force of nature, a self-proclaimed 'Irish Bastard' who has spent years fighting for the rights of Irish women like Philomena. Mari's own story is a tragic embodiment of Ireland's mistreatment of unmarried mothers. Her mother, Josephine, born to an unmarried woman, spent her childhood in an industrial school in Waterford. As a teenager, Josephine was transferred to a Magdalen Laundry in County Cork, where she was forced to work as a seamstress. In 1959, sheltered and naive after a lifetime spent in institutions, Josephine became pregnant and gave birth to Mari in April 1960 in the mother-and-baby home in Bessboro, County Cork. Mari lived in Bessboro with Josephine for eighteen months until she was put on a plane – one of 2,000 Irish babies from Ireland taken from their mothers and sent to America for adoption. During her time in Bessboro, Mari was one of hundreds of infants in mother-and-baby homes across Ireland who were enrolled, without their mothers' consent, as part of a vaccine trial run by the pharmaceutical company Burroughs Wellcome. Later a teenage Mari would become pregnant and be placed in a home for unwed mothers in Philadelphia. She too would surrender her baby, a little girl, for adoption.

I have met Mari many times, and we embrace warmly. She turns to introduce me to Philomena, who is surprisingly tall but leaning heavily on a cane. Behind Philomena is Jane Libberton, her daughter. They both look exhausted.

'Hello, sweetheart, it's nice to meet you,' Philomena says.

She extends her arm to link mine. 'I'm absolutely parched. Would you mind if we get a cup of tea before we start?'

I feel instantly at ease. We move slowly towards the bar, the Hollywood publicist in our wake. Philomena complains about the mediocre tea in America and asks where I'm from. I gently rib her about her impressive entourage.

'Can you believe it?' she chuckles. 'An aul wan like me getting all this attention?'

We sit in a quiet corner of the bar and order tea and sandwiches. Philomena rests her walking stick against the sofa.

'We'll just have a chat, Philomena,' I say.

'Do you want me to start?' she asks. 'Shall I start when my mother dies?'

Suddenly we are interrupted by Jane and Mari, who have sat down to join us. Jane orders a vodka and tonic and takes out a pen. She asks what news organization I am from, noting carefully the details in a small notebook. She seems protective of her mother and I am keen to signal to her that I am not just any journalist, that I am also a secret daughter, like the brother she never knew. But I say nothing. This is about Philomena, I decide, not me.

'Shall I start?' Philomena asks again.

I turn on my tape recorder. Philomena begins to talk. It is clear that she is used to telling her story in this way. She speaks rapidly, barely pausing for air.

'My mother died when I was six years of age and she left six kids, three girls and three boys. Dad kept the three boys at home but he put us girls into a convent school in Limerick. I was there until I was eighteen. My auntie lived in Limerick City so she took me to live with her. One night she took me to a carnival. I had never seen a carnival in my life, all those bright lights after being in the convent all those years. That's where I met up with Anthony's father. And did the deed.'

Jane interrupts. 'It was a night of romance, Mum, that's how we're calling it.'

Philomena laughs. She has a delightful throaty chuckle. She turns to me and winks. 'You're right. It was a night of romance. I was as green as cabbage. Off I went home, not knowing what I had done. I had arranged to meet the young man – his name was John, handsome boy he was too – the next week.

'Come the next week I said to my auntie, "I'm going to meet this boy, John, who I met last week." She said, "Oh no you're not. You're not going out." I told her, "But I've promised him, he'll be waiting for me." She gave me a crack across the face and locked me in. That was the end of John. Never again did I see him. He never knew he was a father.'

My thoughts turn to Sarah, and to another wicked aunt.

Philomena continues. 'And then a few months later my aunt noticed me and she said, "Are you pregnant?" I said, "What's pregnant?" I didn't know what she meant. She got me to the doctor and discovered I was very pregnant and straight away I was taken to the home in Roscrea.

'After the birth I was allowed to nurse Anthony for eight weeks. Then I was sent over to the main building in the convent to work. I was given the laundry. I was there for three and a half years. I could have gotten the kitchen or the garden but the laundry was the warmest place. I stayed there working but every day, from four to five in the afternoon, I was allowed to go and play with my baby. He was adorable. An absolutely adorable child.'

'Did you know that he would be adopted?' I ask.

'In those days, what did I know? You just believed everything you were told and you didn't argue about anything. I reared Anthony for three and a half years. I signed him off in June 1955. They sent for me on a Sunday evening. There was somebody else with the nun, Mother Barbara, a man, I didn't know who he was. They just said, "Sign this form. Anthony is going to be adopted." I didn't even read it. I went from June to December wondering, "Oh my God, when are they going to take him away? Is my baby going? Is my baby going?"'

Up until now, Philomena has been matter-of-fact in telling her tale. But suddenly, her voice catches.

'One day in December this young nun, a nice nun, caught me and said, "Quick, up the stairs!" I remember running up the stairs and looking out the window and there he was going off in the car. I saw his little face, framed in the window. My God in heaven. Can you imagine? I was crying and carrying on and creating such a huge fuss. The nuns said, "Stop your nonsense, you should be grateful you had your boy adopted." I can still feel the pain when I think back on it. Imagine, a little three-year-old boy. He was very loving. A very loving, cuddly little boy. Absolutely adorable. And he was gone, just like that.'

I am fighting tears. I am thinking of my youngest child, a little girl, Neasa, who has just turned two. Neasa is doughy and delicious and the light of our lives. Her capacity for joy and affection is astonishing. She cannot get enough of me, nor I of her.

'Have you seen the movie yet?' Philomena asks.

'Actually, no, not yet,' I say. 'To be honest, I can't get through the trailer without crying. I should probably tell you that I'm adopted too. I think that's why it's too hard for me to watch.'

Philomena turns to me. She takes my hand in hers. 'You should go, sweetheart,' she says. 'It would do you good to cry.'

The publicity woman approaches our table. She looks at

me and taps a manicured nail on to the surface of her watch. I smile and mouth, 'OK.' I have so much to ask. I think about Sarah.

'Can I ask you a little bit about the secrecy?' I venture. 'I know that you didn't tell anyone about Anthony for decades. Can you talk a little about that, about why you didn't tell Jane?'

'We were just so ostracized and so browbeaten,' says Philomena. 'You just believed everything that they told you. It was such shame. My father disowned me. My mother had died. I carried my secret all through my life, for fifty years. It never left me. I kept thinking that I can't tell this to anybody. It's too serious, I've committed a grave sin.'

I nod towards Mari. 'Mari knows my mother's story, Philomena. Her story has some similarities to yours. When I go home to Ireland, I see her but we meet in secret. She has never told anyone about me. Not even her husband or kids. This has been going on for fourteen years. I was born in 1972. My birth mother is living in this shiny new Ireland but she's still afraid to tell the truth.' I pause. 'What would you say to her, if you met her?'

Philomena looks thoughtful. She is still holding my hand. I have abandoned my note-taking. I feel close to the oracle, to the source.

'I would say, please, please, please, will you please come forward and tell your story like I did. I know it took me a long time. I was in the same situation. I was so afraid to tell. In the end it was my brother who made me do it.'

'You were afraid that we would reject you,' says Jane.

'I was,' says Philomena. 'I was. But, of course, I should have known better because they are the most wonderful daughter and son. I should have known better. But the nuns had drummed it into me that I couldn't tell anyone, that I needed to keep it a secret. You were browbeaten so much. Your mother, Caitríona, she would be feeling a lot of guilt.'

'Perhaps I could get my mum to call yours?' Jane suggests. 'Maybe that would help?'

I smile at her, touched by her kindness. 'That would be lovely,' I say.

'Oh, what I could say to your mum,' Philomena says. 'What I could say to her. It is such a relief when it does come out, when you finally tell your story. If only I could tell her that.'

We are interrupted by a waiter who stoops to collect some plates. In the silence, Mari leans across to say something to Jane. Noticing this, Philomena turns away from the other two women. She takes my other hand and looks me straight in the eye. She says something in a whisper that I cannot catch. I lean forward.

'Sorry?' I say.

Philomena speaks again. She is barely audible.

'Do you pray?' she asks. Our heads are almost touching.

I pause. In all of the press articles and movie reviews I have read about Philomena, one fact stands out: her almost superhuman capacity for forgiveness, particularly for the nuns and the Catholic Church who took her little boy away.

I don't want to disappoint her. But locked in Philomena's gaze, I know my only option is to speak the truth.

'No,' I say, shaking my head, 'I don't.'

I feel enormous shame as Philomena searches my face. 'I'm very angry with the Church, Philomena, I'll be honest.'

Philomena frees one of her hands to pat me gently on the arm. She looks determined.

'Then I'll pray for you,' she says. 'And for your mother. That God will give her the grace and the courage to open up. That's what I'll do,' she says.

For the first time in a very long time, I lose my composure. With one hand still in Philomena's, I begin to cry.

Later that afternoon, back at home, I go about my usual order of business, catching up with the kids, checking homework, giving Neasa her bath. But I feel altered, as though I have just received a blessing. I can still feel the warmth of Philomena's hand in mine. I have to fight the urge to cry.

At around 6 p.m., while making dinner, I decide to send Sarah a quick text message. I need to tell her about Philomena. It is eleven o'clock in Dublin but I am guessing that she is still awake.

Just met Philomena and told her about you. She had such empathy for you. Said you are not alone. I wished so much that you could have been there. She has offered to meet you sometime when she's in Ireland. Perhaps we could do that together? Xxxxxxx

Sarah's reply is almost instantaneous.

I have seen her photo in the paper. She looks like a very nice woman. I think it took her fifty years to open up. I'm praying for a miracle for myself. xxxxx

15

30 April 2014

It is three in the afternoon and I am reversing my car out of the narrow driveway of our home in Washington in a torrential rainstorm. I am on my way to pick up Liam and Caoimhe from their school a mile and a half up the road. Behind me, strapped into her car seat, sits Neasa, groggy-eyed after being rudely woken from her nap. I look at the clock and curse my tardiness. In this weather I realize that it will be impossible to find parking close to the school.

My mobile phone beeps with an incoming text message. I pause, but decide to ignore it. The phone beeps again: a second message. I stop the car, still halfway out on the street, and swipe the screen. I assume it's a friend running late who is asking me whether I can collect her child from school, but the text message is from an Irish mobile number that I don't recognize.

> *Hi Caitríona, Siobhán here. My mum has just told me and John about you, I'm delighted to hear I have a sister and can't wait to meet you. We're going to*

The message ends abruptly. I swipe the screen again.

> *have a celebration tonight, such exciting news. Only me and John know so far. Great news xxx*

I reread the message, my brain misfiring wildly. I have seven Irishwomen, all friends, coming to dinner on Friday night. One of them is called Siobhán. Why, I wonder, is Siobhán texting me to tell me that she is my sister? I stare at my phone, as if willing it to speak, to clear up this mystery. Suddenly it hits. The secret is out. There is a sudden and deep fracturing of my thoughts. I stifle a sob, not wanting to startle Neasa, and try to concentrate on getting the car into gear and up the road. I need to get the kids but time has suddenly stopped. At MacArthur Boulevard I make a wrong turn. By now I am hyperventilating. At the next set of traffic lights I stop and take out my phone to call Dan at work. I try to say something when he answers but realize that I have lost the ability to speak. Dan is frantic on the other end thinking that something has happened to the kids. 'They're OK,' I manage to say finally, 'they're OK. It's just . . . it's just that she's told them. Sarah has told her children about me. The secret is out. What am I going to do?'

I turn left on to a side street and make a U-turn. The rain is falling harder now. Half a mile up the road, my phone beeps again. At the next red light I look down at the screen, terrified. It's another Irish number that I don't recognize. I swipe the screen.

Heeeeey Caitríona, it's John here . . . your new brother!! My mam has just told me and my sister Siobhán about you :D. So much to say!!! The three of us are just in Dublin now talking about you :D

Somewhere behind me a car blasts its horn. I look up and see that the light has turned green.

I turn the phone off. I cannot think straight. It's 3.15 and

I'm late for pick-up. I park illegally at the school, unstrap Neasa from the back and run up the stairs. I need to see my kids.

Two days after I had tea with Philomena, I sat down at my computer and wrote a long feature for the *Irish Independent* about our conversation. I intended the article to be an account of the unlikely transformation in Philomena's life since the appearance of the book and the film. But sitting at my laptop, I found myself instead writing about my relationship with Sarah. It was the first time I had ever written about these things for publication and it felt surprisingly cathartic. Rereading the article, I felt satisfied with my version of events. That evening I filed the piece quickly to my editors in Dublin before I could have any second thoughts.

A few days later, before the Philomena piece appeared, an editor on the features desk called in a panic. An Irish celebrity chef had just given an interview about the trauma he endured in 1981 when he and his girlfriend gave up their son for adoption. It was big news, she said, all over the papers. The executive editor wanted an article for the next day's paper by a person who had been adopted as a child. Could I file something quickly, say in two hours? I hesitated. It was Wednesday, one of my stay-at-home days, and I was on the living-room rug playing with Neasa. It would be impossible to write a sensitive piece with a toddler lurching about the house, so I demurred politely. But the editor persisted. Just this once, she pleaded, you would be really helping me out. I relented, silently cursing the facts of the freelancer's life that made it so difficult for me to say no.

The article ran the following day. Logging on to the *Irish Independent*'s website, my stomach lurched when I read the sensational headline that a subeditor had put next to my photograph: 'I was adopted 41 years ago, and my heart has never healed'. I had texted Sarah the previous evening to warn her about the piece. I cringed now thinking about her buying the newspaper, leafing through the pages, her eyes settling on that headline. I picked up my phone and started texting.

You ok over there? Xxxxx

An hour later Sarah replied:

Hi Caitríona . . . I am ok now but my head was spinning for a while. I am so sorry for everything. I really don't know how to undo all the hurt I have caused u. I am the cause of all ur suffering. Sarah xxxxx

I texted her back:

You have not hurt me in any way. It's not your fault, nor do I blame you for anything. I like who I am and my adoption is a huge part of that. I wouldn't change a thing about my life, genuinely. Please don't be so hard on yourself. You are the bravest woman I know, not to mention the light of my life. Xxxxxx

Seconds later, another response:

Thanks so much for being so nice but I know deep down that I have really messed up. I hope u are ok today. Xxxxx

I groaned. I wasn't getting through to her. And this texting back and forth was driving me crazy. I just wanted to pick up the phone, like any normal daughter, and talk to Sarah in person, to bring her back from the ledge. But Sarah had a no-calls-out-of-the-blue policy. I regretted writing that damn article. Whose story was it, anyway? I wasn't sure any more.

Two weeks later the Philomena story ran, a long feature article. I texted Sarah in advance to warn her. Waking up the next morning, I reached across to my bedside table to check my phone. No messages. I knew that Sarah would already have bought the papers. I sent a quick text, asking if she was OK. A couple of minutes later a reply flashed up on my screen.

> *I don't want to lie and say I'm fine but I'm coping. Find it hard to believe I am reading my life story. Don't worry about me. I'm really sorry for all the hurt and pain I have caused you. Xxxxx*

I slipped out of bed and poked my head out into the darkness of the upstairs hallway. Silence from the kids' room. I glanced at my phone. I still had enough time to respond before the mayhem of the morning ensued. I was brimming with anxiety, frightened all of a sudden that Sarah would think this was some dark plot orchestrated to drag her out of the closet. It was not. I wasn't exactly sure what was going on, but I felt altered in the aftermath of meeting Philomena. I needed to tell my story.

I started to type:

> *There's no need to put on a brave face and say that all is fine. I know that this must be incredibly hard for you and I am worried sick that I have gone too far. Please know that I love you and that everything will be fine. This is not a campaign to get you to tell people about me. You have not caused me any suffering. I am happy and whole. My only wish is that you could have some peace of mind too.*
> *Xxxxxxxxxx*

I waited. Half an hour later a message lit up on my phone.

Thanks Caitríona. I admit I am putting on a brave face but I know u need to write about it to cope as well. U have nothing to worry about. U have been wonderful. I'm the one in the wrong. Xxxxx

Over the course of the following days, the comments section on the website beneath the Philomena article was filled with messages from other secret sons and daughters across Ireland. Three days after the piece ran, I got a call from a producer for a morning radio talk show on RTÉ. I had recorded something for the same programme a few days previously but that segment had yet to air. Let's scrap that interview, the producer suggested. How about you come on air and talk about your adoption story instead?

I texted Sarah immediately. For the first time in fourteen years, I asked if I could call her directly. *Don't call*, she replied, *I'll ring you in a couple of minutes*. I imagined her back in Dublin, turning to her husband to say that she needed to pop out to the shops. Twenty minutes later my phone rang. I told Sarah about the radio show.

'I want to discuss this with you before I decide what to do,' I told her. 'I'm worried about the effect that this will have on you. I won't do it if you say so.'

Sarah's voice sounded strong. 'I'm fine, Caitríona, you go for it. I know that this is your way of coping. Go for it, seriously.'

A few days later I went on air. Some weeks previously I had written another feature for my newspaper about Brené Brown, an American scholar who writes about vulnerability and shame. I interviewed her over the phone, listening intently to her compelling pitch: that to live a full and truthful life, we need to be vulnerable, to take emotional risks and show our true selves. Vulnerability takes courage, Brown told me. If you want to find your way back to someone, she said, vulnerability is the path.

It was all a bit American New Age to my cynical Irish ear but, deep down, Brown's message resonated. On the day of the radio interview, sitting in a recording booth at National Public Radio in downtown Washington, I dug deep for courage and tried to channel Brené Brown. I spoke about my adoption, my search for Sarah and our fourteen-year affair. Listening back now to the recording, I am struck by how pained I sound. Towards the end I emphasized how much I loved Sarah and how, in spite of the affair, there would always be a place for her in my life. 'It is not easy being a secret but my love is unconditional and I am always there.'

For two excruciating days I didn't hear from Sarah. I was suffering what Brown calls a 'vulnerability hangover', that terrible feeling that comes when you fear that you've said too much. On the third day, unable to contain my anxiety, I sent a tentative message.

Hope you're still speaking to me and that all is ok. Xxxxxxxxx

Thirteen minutes later came Sarah's reply.

In total shock but will get in touch when feeling better.

Unlike every other text or email she had ever sent, there were no sign-off kisses.

It would be five weeks before I heard from Sarah again. During that time I obsessively checked the death notices in the Irish newspapers, fearing that my publicity binge had sent her over the edge. I was frantic with worry but too afraid to reach out, mindful of Sarah's terse rebuke that she would be in touch when the time felt right. Had she withdrawn from the world entirely, I wondered, or just from me? I reread her text over and over, trying to think past the eleven words on the screen. I wished there was someone in her world who I could call, a friend, a neighbour, anyone to reassure me. The daydream that long haunted me played constantly in my mind: a church full of mourners, a coffin in the centre aisle, the secret daughter in the back row, unseen and alone.

By 30 March, Mother's Day in Ireland, I had had enough. I reached for my phone and sent a brief message:

Happy Mother's Day. Thinking of you Xxxxx.

Sarah's reply was instantaneous:

Thinking of u too. Hope u have a lovely day and the gang spoil u bigtime. Xxxxx.

Exactly one month later, in the kitchen of her Dublin home, Sarah dropped her bombshell on Siobhán and John. It came as a complete shock to me, but when I recovered a bit I remembered that, many years before, Sarah had broached the idea of telling select members of her family in gradual stages. At the time, uncharacteristically frank, I told her it was a terrible idea.

From subsequent conversations, I know that Sarah was not carrying out a premeditated plan when she told Siobhán and John about me. Midway through the afternoon on the day in question, Sarah drove her husband into town so he could catch a train to visit his elderly parents. On the way back home, as her car idled at a traffic light, she considered her options. For weeks, in the wake of my articles and radio appearance, she had experienced trouble sleeping. She was filled with a crushing tiredness, a deadening of her mind. A couple of miles down the road lay a secluded cove and a sandy beach. To her left, tucked behind some narrow streets, was the house where she lived. In the kitchen at that moment, two of her children, now adults, were busy preparing dinner. Gripping the steering wheel, Sarah had a moment of truth. 'I thought to myself,' she would tell me later that night, 'that either I go home and tell them now or I go to the beach and do something stupid.'

Thankfully, Sarah turned her car towards home. Minutes later she was standing in the kitchen in front of two of her kids. She heard herself utter the words, *There is something you need to know.* 'I thought she was going to say that she had cancer,' Siobhán would later tell me. 'I was so relieved when she said, "You have a sister".'

Four simple words: *You have a sister.* The secret was out. The sky didn't fall. The walls didn't crumble. My two siblings thought it was the best thing they had ever heard. Siobhán texted me later that afternoon.

Very emotional here. So strange, I was only saying earlier today how I wished I had a sister and I did all this time. Delighted to hear you exist, Mom says you're gorgeous. I've given her plenty of hugs. She's delighted to have told me and John. A big relief as she has been very agitated recently. Sensed something wasn't right over the past few months but it's great news. Can't wait to meet you. Xx

'Delighted isn't the word. They're over the moon,' Sarah told me later that night when I called her on her mobile phone while she sat celebrating with John and Siobhán. 'They're so, so excited. It was the easiest thing in the world to tell them, the easiest thing in the world. I hadn't planned it.'

Sarah's voice had changed. It was lighter, daintier, the sunniest I had ever heard. I snatched a brief glimpse of an entirely different person. 'I haven't been well,' she said. 'I'm beginning to feel better. I'm beginning to get hungry again.'

Sarah passed the phone to Siobhán, who immediately started crying. Her voice was tentative, quivering. 'I can't believe it,' she kept saying, over and over again. 'Today at work I was telling a cleaner about my family, how I had two brothers but always wanted a sister. Then I come home and about two hours later my mother walks in and tells me that she has a daughter that I don't know about.

'I always knew that something was wrong. This finally feels like the missing piece of the puzzle.'

The morning after the revelation, I drifted about my house, hung over after too many glasses of wine, alive but barely present. All around me, normal life continued. The kids went to school, I went to work. On Friday night, mentally exhausted, I hosted my seven friends for dinner. I sat at the head of the table and watched as they ate and drank and laughed. I felt unmoored from my body, suspended above the table, hovering over us all. I cursed the Palmer stoicism that demands that the show must go on no matter what. I should have cancelled the dinner. All I wanted to do was curl up in a ball and drift away.

The moment that I had been imagining for fourteen years had come and gone. I felt as though I should be walking on air. Instead I was in shock, stunned that Sarah had given Siobhán and John my phone number but never thought to call me first to say that the secret was out. That slight was all I could think about. It was as though I were a child again, voiceless, with no rights. I was given away without any choice. I was hidden away without any choice. Even now, the manner in which I was brought out into the light had nothing to do with me.

On Sunday, four days after the revelation, I finally lost control. In two days' time I was to take a train to New York to attend a fundraising gathering for an adoption institute. The thought of stepping into a room full of adoptees and birth parents filled me with dread, but politeness told me I needed to go. There was a two-hour babysitting gap I needed to fill while I was gone, and I asked Dan if he could come home early from work. He demurred, telling me he had too much work on. 'Isn't there anyone else you can find?' he asked.

All the anger and frustration within me reared up in a flash. My cells felt as though they had caught on fire. Standing in the kitchen, clearing away dishes after lunch, I raised the white ceramic bowl that I was holding in both hands above my head and let it fall with a crash on to the kitchen floor. Dan, who had been in the dining room, ran wide-eyed into the kitchen. He saw the look on my face and ushered the children away. I felt flooded with shame but still my anger refused to abate. I felt, almost with relief, as though I was finally losing my mind.

On my next trip to Dublin, in July, I meet Sarah for lunch at the Marine Hotel. We walk together to the bar area where a large group of women – mostly of Sarah's age – are seated at a rectangular table near the window. They are raucous, squealing like schoolgirls, their heads bent together in what seems like a ferocious exchange of gossip. It is hard to hear above the din. I observe Sarah furtively scanning the group to see if there is anyone she knows. A harried-looking waiter ferries pots of tea back and forth. I direct Sarah to a table drenched in sunlight, across the room from the group of women. I can tell by the look on her face that she would rather sit elsewhere but I am firm in my choice. I want, I need, to assert some control.

Sarah looks lighter than she has in years. She is sleeping much better, she tells me, and feeling less jittery. 'I feel now, with Siobhán and John, that I can offload,' she tells me. 'We talk about you all the time. John keeps asking me, "How did you cope all these years?"'

Her face fills with wonder. 'It was the easiest thing in the world to tell them,' she says again. 'It wasn't planned. I hadn't planned it. And the next thing they're talking to you.' She pauses, furrowing her brow. 'I can't remember. Did they email or call you?'

'They texted me,' I tell her. I haven't confronted her about this. Now she has given me an opening to the subject, but I let it go. I am incapable of confronting her, I realize. Why do I perpetually feel as though I don't have a say in how this story unfolds?

'It was the best night ever,' Sarah says, smiling. 'I was keeping everything hidden in my own life. But this was the best thing I ever did and they were so thrilled. So thrilled.'

'So where do you stand with all of this?' I ask. 'Do you think this is the first step?'

'I do, I do. This is phase one,' Sarah says. 'I would love to offload to the others. I would love to feel free. But I don't. I feel very shackled. I would love to be like you.'

I look at her quizzically. 'Like me?' I ask.

She continues. 'You know? Free. I would love to have everything brand new again. To start all over again.'

The sentence hangs out there until suddenly Sarah clasps her hands to her mouth and turns to me in horror.

'Oh, Caitríona. I didn't mean that. I don't mean that. Of course, I would have had you. It's just . . .'

I take her hand. 'I know what you mean,' I tell her. 'Please. Don't apologize. I know exactly what you mean.'

And I do. For over forty years Sarah has lived a bifurcated life. Internalizing the shame that began the moment she discovered she was pregnant, Sarah has limped through life believing that she is undeserving of happiness and trapped inside a secret. What daughter wouldn't understand a desire to take that pain away, to erase the past and start again?

Sitting here, our hands still entwined, I feel as though we are edging closer to the heart of the matter. I tentatively probe. 'So, is it your husband, is it Michael, that's the issue?'

'Yes, yes, he is. I just feel as though life would return to the way it was after everyone back home found out about you. That I would be back to square one, homeless.'

Can it really be that Sarah believes her husband would react in the same way that her father did over forty years ago? Even after having such a positive experience with Siobhán and John?

'When I would visit home in the years after you were born, there was no talk, total silence. The relationship with my father was good before I fell pregnant. After that, I was totally ignored. I spent years avoiding him. I was dreaming about that, not so long ago. I dreamt that I was home with just my father and I woke up in a cold sweat. I was petrified and I thought, "What am I doing?" And I woke up and I realized, it is only a dream.'

'So are you worried that Michael would treat you the same?'

'Yes,' she says, her lip trembling. 'It's a terrible thing to say, but I am. I'm just worried that he would walk away, just walk away.'

The waiter interrupts to clear our plates. Across the room the women are huddled together in a mass of laughter.

'I'll be sixty-five soon,' Sarah now says, brightening. 'And then I'll be seventy, then seventy-five, then eighty. It's a case of wishing my life away.'

I inhale deeply. 'It's tragic that you feel that way,' I say.

'I know,' Sarah says, 'it's stupid.'

The thought of Sarah trying to rush through her life, to get it over with, fills me with sadness. I wonder how many other women like her, secret birth mothers, carry the same burden?

'No, I'm just delighted that I'm the age I am,' Sarah says. 'That I'm older now. I say, "Another five years, and then another, and then another, and that will bring me up to eighty." And hopefully it won't be long after that. And that's fine.'

On that summer visit to Dublin, and again in the autumn, I met Siobhán and John, and was awed by the graceful way that they welcomed me into their lives. My relationship with them feels natural and firm. Both of them have personalities that are rooted and steady; they stand tall in the world. I look at them and my heart bursts with pride.

In October 2014 I brought Siobhán to Number 49 to meet Liam and Mary. I will never forget that afternoon watching my parents observe Siobhán, the amazement on their faces at seeing my biology reflected up close in the form of another adult.

Once, several years earlier in the parking lot of the Marine Hotel, I had orchestrated a brief meeting between Sarah and Liam. Dad had arrived several minutes early to pick me up and I noticed him, standing next to his car, as I exited the main door of the hotel with Sarah. With a boldness that surprised me, and without turning to ask Sarah's permission, I gestured to Dad to come closer. I stood back and held my breath as my biological mother and adoptive father approached one another, reached out and warmly embraced. There were no tears, no grand declarations. Instead, Sarah and Liam bent their heads towards the other as though they were old friends. The conversation was light and breezy. Sarah, constantly amazed by my reports of Liam's year-round swimming in the Irish Sea, asked whether he'd had a dip that day. (He had.) Liam, who holds a deep reverence for the teaching profession, enquired about Sarah's crop of students that year. I simply stood back and observed these two people, both so dear to me, aware of how natural, how healing, the moment felt.

But later I harboured guilt over Mam's absence from that meeting. Repeatedly, over the years, Mam had extended an open invitation for Sarah to visit and I know it hurt her deeply when Sarah politely refused. Too often, wrapped up in my own feelings, I forgot how the secret had affected my parents, particularly my mother, who has been unfailingly gracious and generous about my long and circuitous journey to find myself.

And so, that day at Number 49, I found my throat catching as I watched Mam take Siobhán's hands in hers and welcome my new sister into our home. 'You're *so* good to drop in,' Mam told her. 'It's *so* lovely to meet you.'

Siobhán and I sat and had a cup of tea with Liam and Mary. Later I took her round the corner for lunch at a local brasserie. Over burgers we chatted about Sarah and the continuing weight of the secret. Soon I became aware that I was referring to Sarah in Siobhán's presence as 'your mother'. I pointed this out and switched prepositions to try the unfamiliar 'our mother'. We both laughed. But the words felt odd, woolly in my mouth. It wasn't working.

When I got back to Number 49 that afternoon, Liam and

Mary met me at the door. They could barely contain their excitement. 'She's a lovely girl,' Liam said. 'So gentle, she reminds me of you. She has a lovely way about her.'

Mam was beaming. 'Such a lovely girl,' she agreed. 'And very like you. She has your build, your eyes. She is a mirror image of you.'

I had never seen her happier.

16

Autumn 2014

Early one morning I kiss Liam and Mary goodbye and drive my rented car through the backstreets of north Dublin, heading for the orbital motorway. I am on a pilgrimage of sorts, to the town where Sarah first met Tom. In my reporter's notebook on the passenger seat next to me is the address of a pub where I am to meet a local man. Days earlier I made contact with this man through a friend of a friend, an editor at a local newspaper. I told the editor that I was writing a book and wanted to interview someone in the town who had lived there during the early 1970s. He recommended John Gallagher, an amateur historian. I phoned John and gave him an edited account of my quest. I know that Tom still lives in the town and I feel duty-bound to protect his privacy.

I arrive at the pub ten minutes early, order a pot of tea and some toast and sit in a darkened corner. The room smells of stale beer and looks dreary in the low light. Garish bunting is draped across the low red ceiling. I am the only customer until John arrives, a tall man with lively eyes, bearing books laden with photographs depicting the town over the past century. He is brimming with enthusiasm. He has lived in the town his entire life, he tells me, and is eager to help. Without naming any names, I outline to John the details of Tom and Sarah's romance. I describe the boarding house where Sarah stayed, the name of the bar where they met. John nods enthusiastically. He knows all the spots.

While I scribble furiously in my notebook, he takes me back in time.

In October 2010, I had come across Tom's name, listed next to Aileen's, in the comments section of a wedding-video website. The brief clip on the site appeared to be from the wedding of Tom's daughter, my half-sister. It was an extraordinary discovery: the internet gods had delivered moving images of my birth father and my paternal half-siblings for my vicarious viewing pleasure. The opening shot was of a modest suburban house that I assumed belonged to Tom. A couple of seconds later came a close-up of a smiling bride who looked uncannily like me across the eyes.

I felt like a stalker, but part of me was too excited to care. I had never seen an image of my birth father and here he was, in a rented morning suit, walking his other daughter up the aisle. He looked nervous and tense. He was shorter, stockier, fairer than I had imagined. There was less of the swagger about him than Sarah's stories had implied. He appeared almost vulnerable.

Now, sitting in the darkened bar with John, I think about the wedding video. I know what I am working towards. Tom's home address is in my notebook. I wonder if it matches the front of the house that the camera lingered over briefly in the wedding video. I wonder if I have the courage to go there, just to see it for myself. Nothing more. I pause, wondering if I can trust John. We have been talking for over an hour and a half.

Finally I confide in John and tell him my birth father's name. The moment feels good, cleansing. I let the name float out there, waiting for John's reaction.

John's face remains expressionless. He is thoughtful.

'Ah yes,' he says. 'I wouldn't know him very well. I see him about the town every now and then. Quiet man.'

I am taken aback. The image I have of Tom is of a tearaway driving through the town in his sports car, his wide-collared shirt buttoned down low, leaving a trail of destruction in his wake.

'Would you say that he's a good man?' I ask.

'I would, I would,' John says. 'A family man. Quiet. Hard-working.'

I open my notebook to the page where I have recorded Tom's address. I push it towards John.

'I believe this is where he lives,' I say. 'I was half thinking of driving past. Not to go in, obviously. Just to take a look.'

John squints at the address. 'I know exactly where that is,' he says. 'I need to head that way in a while. Why don't you follow me in your car?'

I pay the bill and we head out into the car park. Standing next to his car, his keys in his hands, John has a sudden change of mind. He suggests that we postpone the drive momentarily so he can show me the boarding house where Sarah once lived. We cross the busy main street and stand outside a handsome red-brick house set behind a high wall. I look through the wrought-iron gate and see the ghosts of my past swarming forth. A bit further on, John pauses outside a large whitewashed building that is under reconstruction. It is the old singing lounge where Sarah used to meet Tom. I poke my head inside the door. The floor is strewn with saw-dust and planks of wood and there are workers milling about, but I see snippets of its former grandeur, tall arches and a wide mahogany-capped staircase. I am captivated. A friendly worker behind the front desk asks if she can help. I smile and shake my head.

'I'm just taking a quick look. My parents used to come

here when they were dating,' I tell her. John looks at me with wide eyes. I back away.

We return to our cars. By now a misty rain has begun to fall. I follow John's car through the gloom and weave of the town. The narrow pavements are teeming with pedestrians. We turn right up a hill and take several twisty turns. John pulls into the car park of a church next to the community centre where his historical society meets. Across the way is a housing estate. I recognize it as the one from the wedding video.

I park next to John's car. He gets out and we stand together in the rain. He nods towards the estate: 'That's where he lives.'

I thank John for his kindness and shake his hand. John releases his grip, opens his arms and we embrace.

'Look after yourself now,' he says. 'And try not to take all of this to heart.'

'I won't,' I say. 'My kids keep me grounded. This will all work out.'

John smiles, says goodbye and walks away. Suddenly I can barely muster the energy to look for Tom's house. I am still trying to process the phantoms I saw a few moments ago in the town. I need to take stock, to sit alone for a moment. Inside the car I turn the ignition and crank up the heat. I am shivering in the dampness.

A moving shape to my right causes me to look up. I see John standing next to my window. I open the door. John is smiling.

'I've just thought of something,' he says, gesturing with his hand. 'Come with me.'

We walk towards the community centre. John opens a narrow door and we descend into a basement. Walking along a corridor, we pass a kitchen and step into an office lit by flickering fluorescent lighting. Across the room an elderly woman works on a computer.

'How are yeh, Mary?' John calls. The woman looks up and smiles at us both.

'Grand, thanks, John,' she says, returning her gaze to her screen. I am relieved when John doesn't make introductions.

He sits down at an old desktop computer and turns it on. We wait as it whirrs into life. John starts to click open folders of black-and-white photos. I recognize some from the large books that John had shown me in the bar.

John scrolls through the photos one by one. Images swim into view – families lined up outside house fronts, religious processions through the town, First Holy Communicants standing outside a church front. I have no idea what he is looking for.

'Here we are,' John says under his breath. He is now scrolling through a bunch of wedding photographs: lots of long hair and wide collars.

John looks over his shoulder at Mary. She remains fixated on her screen. He puts his index finger to his lips to indicate silence. He quickly scrolls through some images and chooses one. It is a colour photo of a wedding party, nine people in total, sitting on benches in the garden of a hotel. John points his cursor on the face of a young man standing behind the bride and looks at me. I shrug, not understanding.

'That's him,' he mouths silently at me. 'That's Tom.'

I feel a jolt of electricity. Judging by the verdant blooms in the background, it is a summer wedding. John's folder said 1971. I am staring at my birth father in the summer I was conceived. He is broad-shouldered, handsome, his fair hair swept low across his forehead. He stares at the camera, unsmiling but with a jaunty confidence. I can see what all the fuss was about.

John moves his cursor, pointing to the groom. 'That's his brother,' he mouths.

It all makes sense. Sarah had once told me that Tom's brother had married a local girl in the summer of 1971.

He points his cursor to the elderly people flanking the bride and groom. 'Those are his parents.'

I stare at my paternal grandparents. My grandmother looks diminutive and sweet. My grandfather looks fierce. This rush of imagery is almost too much. My heart is beating wildly.

I look at John, mouth, 'Wow,' and wipe some imaginary sweat off my forehead.

John winks at me and again puts his index finger to his lips. He calls Mary over.

'Mary, so where would this man be now?' he asks, pointing his cursor over the face of my uncle, the groom.

'Well now,' Mary says, peering over her glasses at the screen. 'He and his family moved away some time ago.' She mentions the name of another county.

'I'm not sure about this other fellow,' John says, pointing to my birth father.

'But, John, that's Tom _____,' Mary says, looking at the photograph. 'Sure he's local. He married Aileen _____. Lives just down the street.'

Back outside in the parking lot, stunned, overwhelmed, I hug John one more time.

'I feel like I'm chasing ghosts,' I tell him. 'That was unbelievable.'

'It's funny but when I walked away from you it just hit me that I might have these photos,' John says. 'It makes me happy that you saw them.'

I think of Josephine, and now John: total strangers generously helping me on this quest.

'I'm glad you came back,' I say as John escorts me towards my car. 'You're like a guardian angel.'

Minutes later I am driving around the housing estate looking for Tom's house. In the misty rain I struggle to locate the street names and have to reverse several times to make the same loop again. A man in his front garden, inexplicably cutting the grass in the rain, raises his head and stops to stare as I drive past for a third time. I feel exposed, a stalker, clearly up to no good. I worry that someone is going to call the Gardaí. I park the car, frustrated, and pull out my phone. Cursing the slow internet connection, I search for the wedding video of Tom's daughter. Finally I find it, hit play and let it roll. I pause the video when the shot of Tom's house comes into view.

I start the car again, making my way back along the first street. Suddenly I see it on the left, a house that I had passed twice already. I park the car on the right-hand side of the street, several doors down, and check my phone. The picture on the phone matches the house. I shut off the engine and stare at the front door. Now what?

For the first time since entering this town several hours before, the ghosts in my mind quieten. I feel bizarrely at peace. I sit behind the wheel of my rented car and regard my birth father's house. It is an ordinary house, neat and tidy with a row of potted plants arranged on the porch and a small car parked in the driveway. There is a light on inside the hallway and a gentle hum about the place that suggests to me that someone is at home. But I feel no compulsion to march up the driveway and knock on the door. I feel no need to announce myself to the people within. It is enough to just sit here and observe. I feel sorry for Tom, for all that he is missing.

I look at the clock on my phone. My work here is done. It is time to head back to Dublin. I start the car and realize that Tom's house sits in a cul-de-sac: I need to turn the car round. I put the car in gear and drive towards Tom's house. I turn the car ever so slightly into his driveway, pause for several seconds and then reverse back into the street. I drive towards the main road, looking in the rear-view mirror as Tom's house recedes behind. I realize that I am smiling broadly.

In some way, no matter how inconsequential and petty, I have marked my territory.

The visit to the town where Sarah met Tom was, in fact, the second pilgrimage I made in October 2014. I made the first, to Sarah's home village, in the company of Dad.

Liam Palmer has been one of the greatest blessings of my life. Our bond is almost psychic, transcending blood and bones, stronger than any DNA. Growing up, I spent most of my childhood in a perpetual state of anxiety, terrified that, at any moment, Liam could die. I barely let him out of my sight, constantly obsessing about his health, hovering by his side at all times. One scorching summer afternoon, when I was about seven years old, seized with a premonition that I could not explain, I refused to join my aunt and cousins for a play date on Dollymount Strand. Eventually I was forced to go along, but I spent the whole time fretting and looking at the clock, pestering my aunt as to when she would take me back. We returned home that evening to find an ambulance parked outside Number 49 and Liam, on a stretcher, being carried away. It turned out to be nothing more than a severe case of kidney stones and Liam, healthy and smiling, was back home soon. But the intuition I felt that day has stayed with me my whole life. It was as though Liam and I communicated on a cellular level.

For fourteen years I stayed away from the village where Sarah grew up, holding out hope that my first visit there would be in her company. We discussed the possibility several times together, brainstorming how we could pull off such an audacious act while still keeping our relationship under wraps. Once, Sarah suggested that I rent one of the little holiday cottages dotted along the outskirts of the village. We could coordinate, she suggested: plan your trip around a weekend when I am there. I mulled the idea over and over, imagining Sarah arriving for dinner at the cottage, handing her a glass of wine as we sat outside in the evening light and watched the kids play. I had yet to engage in such simple pleasures with Sarah – to cook her a meal, to welcome her into my home – and the holiday cottage fantasy was extremely appealing.

But it never happened. Our world was the bar in the Marine Hotel. It would be ludicrous, I realized, to take our affair back to the village, to sneak around under the noses of her family. And it would only highlight the inequality of our relationship. I hated being an object of shame, hated that I was someone to be hidden away.

And so, I told Sarah of my plans to visit her home village, but I did not specify dates. At the last minute, I asked Dad if he wanted to come along. I figured that if I was to skulk around Sarah's old home then it would help to have a partner in crime. 'We can pretend that we're tourists,' I told him. Dad, always up for an adventure, agreed to come.

On the approach to Sarah's village, the road narrows, hugged by stone walls covered with brambles that shadow our way. A printout of a map that my sister Siobhán created especially for the trip sits in my pocket. It is lovingly put together, outlining all of the family landmarks including the old stone house where Sarah grew up and the homes of

Sarah's various siblings. As I drive deeper into the village, I see Sarah's childhood home exactly where she and Siobhán said it would be, perched on the corner, facing the sea. It is more beautiful than I could have imagined. Rose brambles, lovingly tended, climb the whitewashed walls. Square windows, set deep into the stone walls, are polished and pristine. A large dog lies across the threshold, basking languidly in the late autumnal sun.

We park the car near a seaside pub and walk back towards the village. It is unusually warm for October and the pub terrace is full of people drinking lager in the sun. I look at the faces and search for physical similarities. I see none. We stroll the narrow lanes, pretending to be tourists, snapping pictures as we go. A group of Germans pass in a camper van and wave cheerily to us.

It feels good to be here. Almost natural, almost like coming home.

'It's peaceful here,' Dad says, looking around, 'very peaceful.'

'I know,' I reply, turning my head to gaze out towards the sea. 'I can hardly imagine what it must have felt like to have to leave here and not come back.'

We approach the old stone house. Without thinking, I pause and sit on the stone wall that surrounds it, beneath the shadow of a tall hedge. I rub my hands along the hew of the stones, imagining the men of my family who built it over a hundred years ago. The hedge keeps us hidden but through the leaves I can hear a bustle from within the house, the banging of pots and pans, the low murmur of voices on a radio. A little boy with red hair and big freckles cycles past. Slung over the handlebars of his bike is a clear plastic bag containing a bag of sugar, just purchased at the local store, and no doubt being brought home for the tea. He grins at us as he cycles past and I wink in return. Is he a cousin of mine?

For five minutes we sit companionably on the wall. The late-afternoon sun casts long shadows across the fields. Dad and I are silent but easy in each other's company. The mood is calm, reflective. I have not felt this much at peace in a long time.

'Would you mind me asking . . .' Dad says finally. 'I mean . . .' He pauses. 'I'm sorry to ask this, but do you find this sad or emotional?'

I glance to my right. Dad is looking at me, tentative. There is so much depth to this man, I realize, so many layers. I look at him and my heart bursts with love and gratitude.

'I find it sad,' I tell him. 'It's so beautiful here and yet so much tragedy has happened. I'm sad that this place has been ruined for Sarah; that she rarely visits. I'm sad that her life has turned out the way it has.'

I turn and gaze again at the house. From this angle all I can see are the slate-grey tiles of the roof and the uppermost reaches of the second floor. This belongs to me, I think, and yet it is also denied to me. The people inside this house are my closest blood relatives, the wall that I sit on has been built by my own forebears, and yet here I am, skulking, on the outside, a stranger.

A lone walker in the distance traces the curve of the bay. The cows in the fields across the road are still, their heads bent in the lush grass. The sun is sinking lower in the sky. 'Shall we head back?' Dad asks.

Driving away from the village, the sea at our backs, we round a corner and see an old stone church. I spied it on the way in and felt a tug as we passed. Now, approaching the corner again, I put my indicator on and pull in to the side of the road.

'Do you mind if we stop here for a second, Dad?' I ask.

Beneath the stone church sits a graveyard, cut high into the hill. It is ringed by tall hedges, ochre in the autumnal sun. As we approach the iron gate, a bank of pewter clouds passes low above our heads, momentarily blocking the sun. We make our way in. The hillside is dotted with tall Celtic crosses. There are a few other people here, mostly tourists.

We start at the bottom and begin to work our way up. The ground is soft and clumpy and I worry about Dad, extending a hand to him as we clamber about. As I weave my way through the field of etched stone, I begin to see Sarah's family name. A shiny black marble headstone lists the names of a great uncle and aunt. A couple of rows away I find a cousin, another aunt. I climb higher and higher, Dad by my side, scanning each grave.

At the uppermost extent of the cemetery, in a secluded corner, I find what I am looking for: the grave of my grandparents, Seán and Mairéad. The stone is white marble, the names etched in black, and the bed beneath the headstone littered with tiny white and grey marble gravel. The grave is clean and well cared for, save for a fresh dewy cobweb resting beneath the arch of the cross. I look at Dad and gesture to where I am standing. With wonder he begins to read aloud the writing on the headstone. Hearing my father pronounce the names of my biological grandparents with such tenderness, I am overcome with emotion. It is a moment of pure communion. The secret grandchild has returned.

We are silent for some time. Finally Dad turns to me and gently asks, 'Shall we say a prayer?' I nod and watch as he makes the sign of the cross. I sit on the edge of the grave and close my eyes and think of my grandparents deep below.

'Hello,' I whisper to them in my mind. 'I'm Caitríona, your first-ever grandchild. You've never met me but I thought I would drop by to say hello. This is my dad, Liam. I've had a wonderful life, a privileged life. But I'm here to tell you about Sarah, who has suffered so very, very much since I was born. She is in pain, real pain, and doesn't deserve any of this. Please help her. Please forgive her. I know you do. You just need to tell her.'

Sitting here, above my grandparents, I feel serene and calm. It feels right to be here, alongside the people to whom I belong, those resting beneath me and the man standing by my side. I have made peace with my ancestors and invoked their help. Perhaps my silent prayer will burrow through the fertile soil of this magical place and find its way to Sarah's heart.

I stand up and lean over to gently wipe away the cobweb on the gravestone and allow my hand to linger on the curve of the marble in the sun. Bending down, I pick up three tiny pebbles from the grave and push them deep into the pocket of my jeans, patting my leg and feeling them snug against my hand. I look up and see that Liam has begun to make his way down the sloping graveyard, heading towards the iron gate. I caress the top of the headstone one final time and follow in my father's wake.

Afterword

Once, when Caoimhe was five years old, she sidled up next to me as I sat drafting this book on my laptop. 'What are you doing?' she asked.

'I'm writing a story.'

'What's the story about?' Caoimhe persisted.

I paused, wanting to be honest but also not knowing how to explain the complexities of this narrative to a child so young. 'Well,' I said finally, 'it's a story about a woman, a lovely woman in Ireland who once had a baby but had to give it away.'

'Did she ever get her baby back?' Caoimhe asked.

'She didn't,' I told her. 'The baby grew up and found the woman again and they became friends. But the woman was never able to *really* get her back.'

Caoimhe held my gaze for a while and nodded before looking away. 'That's a sad story, Mommy,' she said, 'a very sad story.'

Beautiful, perceptive Caoimhe is right. This is a sad story. And it is nothing but sadness that compelled me to write this book, to put the story down on paper. This book is by far the most perilous thing I have ever done. The stakes are high and they keep me awake at night. I fear that I may lose Sarah for ever, that she will feel betrayed by things I have written. I fear that I will infuriate the new siblings I have just found, and alienate the sibling I have yet to meet. I worry that by writing so honestly about the pain of adoption, the sense of dislocation that has haunted me my entire life, I may devastate Liam and Mary. I worry what my children will think when they are old enough to read this book.

Many times, especially during moments of paralysing anxiety, I considered walking away from this project. Somehow I have stood firm. I feel, with every fibre of my body, that it is my duty to tell this story and that I will feel diminished if I do not. Writing this book has been my attempt to create order out of chaos, to etch a coherent narrative out of sorrow and pain. At the same time, I have always felt that there is a real sense in which this is not just my story but the story of every other secret son or daughter. This is not just Sarah's story but the story of every other woman who once had a child outside of marriage and gave that child away. This is Liam and Mary's story, and that of every adoptive parent. It is also the story of any person who has lived a life unknowingly tainted by the toxicity of a lingering family secret.

When I sat down to write this book, I thought it might end with a passage summarizing why Sarah kept – and continues to keep – my existence a secret. In my mind it was an open-and-shut case. There was the Catholic Church, with its culture of institutional dishonesty and shame, and the Irish state, which allowed the Church to dictate the terms on which unmarried mothers and their children were treated. There was Irish society, which turned its head the other way, choosing not to see. Less abstractly, there were some obvious villains close to hand – Sarah's aunt, and the neighbour in her home village – who set the machinery of shame in motion, leaving an indelible mark on Sarah's conscience.

But when it comes to family secrets, nothing is ever entirely clear. I cannot explain why Sarah continues to keep me a secret because I simply do not know. Where does fear come from? I am not sure that she knows herself.

That then leaves another reason for writing this book: to publicly exonerate Sarah, my beautiful, broken mother, and to leave a written record for her husband, should he ever find out the truth. Although Sarah believes that she alone is to blame for all that has happened, the facts in this book indicate otherwise.

I do not know for how much longer Sarah can sustain her secret. Should the day arrive when the truth is fully unleashed and Sarah's husband asks how his beloved wife of over thirty years could have kept a secret from him for so long, I pray that this book will help to ease his pain.

Acknowledgements

My family represents the heart of this book and so it is to them that I first turn to express thanks. I am eternally grateful to my parents, Liam and Mary Palmer, for their love, devotion and sacrifice. I am grateful too for their patience and understanding throughout the sometimes painful process of writing this book. I love them both with all of my heart.

My thanks too to my siblings, Thérèse and David, for their love and kindness and for putting up with me for all these years. The little baby girl that Thérèse so longed for has grown up to become her greatest admirer; and my sister's steadfast belief in this book has sustained me throughout the darkest times. My brother, David, has been a life-long friend and an unending source of inspiration. My gratitude also to Paul Byrne and Deborah Haylett, and to my remarkable nieces and nephews, Claire, Sarah, Niamh, Finn, Kitty and Cal.

My dear friend Molly McCloskey, a writer of exceptional talent, was the catalyst who made this book happen. I am lucky to have her in my life. Without Molly I would never have met my agent, Lucy Luck, nor my editor at Penguin Ireland, Brendan Barrington. With great conviction, Lucy took a chance on an unknown writer with just a kernel of an idea. Along the way she offered valuable advice, unflagging enthusiasm and much-needed support.

Now, having written this book, I fully understand why Brendan Barrington is so renowned in the publishing world. It was a joy and an honour to work with him. Not only did Brendan's editorial brilliance and razor-sharp pencil transform this manuscript, but he treated my story – and those I love – with the respect and care they deserve. My thanks too to the entire Penguin Ireland team, especially Cliona Lewis, Michael McLoughlin and Patricia McVeigh. I am grateful also to the copy-editor, Karen Whitlock, for pointing out the rough spots, to Chantal Noel, and to Megan Witt for her fabulous photographic eye.

I owe so much to my extended family, especially my aunt Carmel Palmer, who was an enthusiastic champion of this book from the get-go. Both she and Patricia (Pat) Palmer lent valuable time in recollecting the past. So too did Bríd and Fergus Rush, who gave me the gift of a second family, and Maire Brougham, who lent so much support. I am grateful also to Carmel, Eleanor, Gerald and Tony Wyse, and to Jack King and his late wife, my beloved fairy godmother, Noleen. My thanks too to Angela and Larry Kearney, to Caroline and Keith Palmer, and to Rachel, Stephen and Terence Palmer and their families, lifelong friends all. I remain indebted to my friend Father Hugh Fagan CSSp., who long ago taught me the importance of living each day with gratitude.

I owe so much to the De Luce family, in particular Richard De Luce and his gentle and beautiful wife, Joanne, whose absence has left a giant hole in our hearts. My heartfelt gratitude goes to Amy, Ted, Dave and Anne and the entire De Luce and Eigner clans. My thanks also to Joan Cobble for her friendship and support.

Many passages in this book are built upon interviews, correspond-ence and conversations with people who I am unable to name for fear of revealing the identities of my biological parents. To each and every one of you I express profound gratitude. You courageously opened doors that had been locked for over four decades. I am thankful also to many other people who offered invaluable glimpses of the past, includ-ing Lena Griffin (née Crean), Charlotte Keery, Philomena Lee, Jane Libberton, Susan Lohan, Hilary Piper (née McDonnell), Mari Steed, Ruth Stokes and Heather York. I owe an intellectual debt – and more – to Claire McGettrick for her graciousness in the face of my multiple requests for information and for sharing her accumulated knowledge of the complicated history of adoption in Ireland. Conall Ó Fátharta's remarkable investigative journalism inspired me along the way. My thanks also to Catriona Crowe at the National Archives of Ireland and to Noelle Dowling at the Dublin Diocesan Archives. Geraldine Kierse Irwin lent me her extraordinary library of Irish feminist literature and Professor Jeffrey Huang at Georgetown University secured me one magical book. Professor Lindsey Earner-Byrne of University College Dublin provided valuable insights and friendship. Her book, *Mother and Child: Maternity and Child Welfare in Dublin, 1922–60*, was instrumental in my own research. I will be for ever indebted to Christine O'Hare, who was a constant source of friendship, strength and wisdom. Fellow adoptees Bill Baroni, Heather Katz, Crissy Keen and Christine Koubek shared understanding and more.

The majority of this book was written at the Writers Room DC, my home away from home. I will always be grateful to Alexander and Charles Karelis for opening the door to this wonderful haven and to the many inspirational friends that I made there.

I have been very lucky in my editors and colleagues at the *Irish Independent*, both present and past, especially Kim Bielenberg, Cormac Bourke, Frank Coughlan, Nick Kelly, Gene McKenna, Gemma O'Doherty and Rowena Walsh. The spirit of my friends Peter Carvosso and Nick Doughty runs through these pages. Among many other indispensable lessons, Peter long ago taught me the value of a 'good yarn' while Nick showed me what it is like to live a life with integrity and courage. I miss them both terribly. I also owe thanks to my many friends in the press and diplomatic corps in Washington and abroad who lent support, including Julian Borger, Kevin Conmy, Richard Downes, Norman Houston, Lara Marlowe, Stewart and Suzanne Matthews, Maeve O'Beirne, Caitríona Perry, Robert Shortt, Demetri Sevastopulo and Denis Staunton. I am so grateful to Simon Carswell for his guidance and time. At the World Bank Group, I owe thanks to all of my colleagues but especially Laura Mecagni, Elizabeth Price and Irina Sarchenko for their friendship and support.

Steve Luxenberg, author of the remarkable *Annie's Ghosts*, gave me early and invaluable advice. So too did literary agents Lynn Franklin and Howard Yoon. Mary Challinor offered valuable insights on cover design. Fellow writers Alison Buckholtz, Ada Calhoun, Siobhán Campbell, Mary Costello, Nazila Fathi, Joshua Horwitz, Kathleen MacMahon, Lia Mills, Ramita Navai, George O'Brien and Matteo Pistono offered counsel and support. I was also lucky in the many friends and colleagues who read my manuscript in various forms, including Barbara Ayotte, Julianna Evans, Madeline Johnson, Joseph Rebello, Kimberly Stephens, Eric Weiner and Alexandra Zapruder.

In Bosnia, encircled by the ghosts of Srebrenica, I finally understood the need to search for Sarah. I would never have had the courage to go to Bosnia had it not been for the inspiration of Professor Cynthia Simmons at Boston College. I would never have made it to Boston

College had it not been for the support of Dr Margaret MacCurtain OP. At BC, Cynthia and her colleagues Mariela Dakova, the late Adele Dalsimer and the late Father William B. Neenan SJ showered me with kindness. On my return to Boston, Samantha Power urged me to knock on PHR's door. The many friends that I made there inspire me still.

During the writing of this book, so many friends opened their homes and their hearts or provided diversions and support. Others helped keep the De Luce/Palmer trains running on time. They include Kristin Allstadt, Nancy Arbuthnot, Gail Bailey, Karima Benamri, Kristen and George Beronio, Erin Brooks, Greg and Julianna Caplan, Walker Carter, Vanessa Carswell, Rebecca Cooper, Chris Conway, Janice DeRosa, Mariama Diouf, Lorraine Docherty, Jean Duff, Sabine Durier, Julie Hayes, Nancy Hoover, Jane Jamieson, Serene Jweied, Vanessa Karlo, Francis Laryle, Tanya Scobie Oliveira, Stephanie and Raymond Quianzon, Sandie Quinn, Heather Schwager, Niraj Shah, Amy and Mike Shapiro, Marsha Stalcup, Daniel Street, Jason and Sarah Tama, Gerard Toal, Alvaro Trenchi, Mary and Ted Tschudy, Anne and Charlie Yonkers and Linda Xiaole-Wang. I owe special thanks to Olga Simmonds who has done so much for my family, particularly little Neasa. And to Lela Ivankovic for always being there. Janet Cook Carter supplied an endless run of school pick-ups and a multitude of kindness. Sandra Johnson was there at the very beginning and Dr Thomas Connelly swooped in when it was all done. Susan and Pete Smith showered my family with generosity and took in Liam as one of their own. Jeff Koch and Patty Stolnacker offered friendship and so much more. On the other side of the pond, Deborah Behan, Joe Brazil, Valerie McArdle, Mairéad O'Driscoll, Philip Rogan and Monika Stedul kept the home fires burning.

Maryetta Andrews-Sachs taught me how to dig for courage and the truth. In Boston and Bosnia, Christopher Turpin kept me anchored with love. Dervala Hanley offered inspiration and the promise of a book-lined cottage. Steven Gibson and Courtney Smith were there in big ways and small. Jens and Petra Hanefeld provided second homes in Washington, Berlin and Provence. Corrie Shanahan was my greatest champion and an indefatigable source of encouragement. Kate Yonkers and Kelly Welch sustained me with an abundance of fierce loyalty and love.

In many ways, this book is about courage and truth, and one friend in particular is the embodiment of both. Professor James M. Smith's determination to give voice to Ireland's 'disappeared' – the 30,000 women incarcerated in the shameful Magdalen laundries – helped inspire this book and gave me resolve when my own courage failed. Jim's immensely important book, *Ireland's Magdalen Laundries and the Nation's Architecture of Containment*, was critical to my own research. I cannot repay Jim, or his wife Beatriz Valdez, for their endless kindnesses over two decades. It is a privilege to be their friend.

In April 2014, my life changed for ever when Sarah revealed my existence to two of her children. I am indebted to my new siblings for their grace, their generosity, and for the way that they have embraced me with open arms. My life is immeasurably richer with their presence and I hope that we can continue on the tentative but loving journey that we have begun.

Growing up, I often felt incomplete, adrift between the two dominant strands of my life: the adopted child and the biological stranger without a name. Writing this book has allowed me to weave these combined narratives together, to merge two histories into one. It has also reinforced the reality that my life is now dedicated to one singular truth: my role as mother to Liam, Caoimhe and Neasa, the three miracles who bring me indescribable joy. Every day I look at each of you and my heart bursts with wonder, love and pride. Facing the future, I know this to be true: that with you three in my life, I am more than complete.

My husband, Dan De Luce, has been by my side throughout this entire journey. I could not have asked for a better travelling companion. This book is mine alone but it reflects Dan's remarkable integrity, his steadfast judgement and his singular, unshakeable love. When I needed courage and a friend, I turned first to Dan. I will be forever grateful to him for all that he has given me, in particular his wonderful son, Ivan, who has brought so much joy and laughter into our lives. With you in my life, Dan, every day is a gift.

Finally, Sarah, you showed tremendous courage in allowing me to share our story for this book. That bravery will undoubtedly bring comfort and resolve to so many other secret birth mothers. I want nothing more in this life than to be able to take away your pain and to stand tall, surrounded by those we love, and acknowledge you as my mother. That day may never come, but my devotion to you remains the same. My door, my life, is always open. I love you so very, very much.